MEET THE GREEK
TESTAMENT

MEET THE GREEK TESTAMENT

TWO ESSAYS AND A DIALOGUE
INTENDED FOR THOSE WHO
HAVE LITTLE OR NO GREEK

by

ADAM FOX
Canon of Westminster

SCM PRESS LTD
56 BLOOMSBURY STREET
LONDON

First published November 1952

Printed in Great Britain by
Northumberland Press Limited
Gateshead on Tyne

CONTENTS

Part III

PHILOLOGUS: OR THE WORDS
A DIALOGUE REPORTED

PREFACE

VERY few people now know Greek. Even among the clergy there are many who have not enough of it to be of much use. And I have felt for a long time that it would be worth while to try and write a book explaining to people who know no Greek what kind of things a knowledge of Greek enables you to learn about the New Testament and the Christian religion. I did not wish merely to tell in English what I had learnt from the Greek, but to show what use a student of the New Testament can make of Greek. On reflection this seemed to entail three different attempts. I might begin by explaining how the books of the New Testament came to be written, and what it is that makes me think (as I do) that the Greek text which is the basis of our English translation is for all practical purposes, and in fact almost word for word, just what the Apostles and Evangelists wrote. Secondly, I might try and explain how I can feel fairly sure that I can translate the Greek correctly, and to what sources I go in order to determine the meaning of the text at any particular place. But these two matters would only be preliminary to discussing the most important Greek words and their precise meaning in the Church and out of it. For it is only on the foundation of such exact knowledge that the doctrines of Christianity can be rightly stated and rightly understood.

When I came to make this threefold attempt I soon found that what I was really at was to write a considerable series of short philological articles, preceded by as much information as anyone would need to be master of who was to read—and appreciate—the philology. I discovered also by simple experiment that articles on philology, short or long, are apt to be tedious. You have therefore in the following pages a work which is not all of a kind. It consists of two Essays and a Dialogue. The essays are on the Transmission and the Interpretation of the Greek Testament and seek to convey what the reader needs to know, if he is to find pleasure and instruction in the Dialogue. The subject of the Dialogue, which is on a larger scale, is the philology of some leading words in the Greek Testament, using philology in a wide sense.

It may seem odd to use a dialogue for this purpose. But at least I have the authority of Plato who in his *Cratylus* has presented a long discussion on the origin of language; and in our own literature I can cite the precedent of Horne Tooke's *Diversions of Purley*, that early work on philology, where in dialogue form he attempted a scientific account of the Parts of Speech. Of course it would be ridiculous for me to claim to emulate Plato's graceful conduct of a dialogue, but I believe that I have succeeded in being more life-like than Horne Tooke, which is perhaps not saying very much. It will be seen that the dialogue is in narrative and not in dramatic form. It might be thought that it would be more cumbrous to relate a discussion than simply to assign the words to the different speakers as in a play. But experience shows that this is not so. Plato, in what are perhaps his three greatest works, the *Republic*, the *Symposium*, and the *Phaedo*, professes to have the talk retold to a sympathetic listener, and this is true also of the *Protagoras*, and of the difficult *Parmenides*, where one Cephalus is represented as narrating a long discussion which he had heard repeated by Antiphon who had it at second hand from Pythodorus who was actually present on the original occasion, which must have been some forty years before, if it was all as Plato says. But of course the *Parmenides* is no more history than the dialogue in a historical novel. It is true to life in another sense.

I believe mine is in places rather a teasing dialogue, but so were Plato's. At any rate I hope my imitation of the master's method, however far it falls behind him, may turn out not too bad a way of communicating to the Greekless something of Christianity in Greek.

In writing what follows I owe so much to so many that acknowledgments are impossible. I have given the sources where I could. That I owe much to Bishop Lightfoot and Bishop Westcott will be obvious, and I wish to name with particular gratitude Sanday and Headlam's commentary on *Romans*, where I so often find just what I want to know.

I began writing this book for the benefit of a young gentleman named Alan Coldwells, and in the writing it was called *Alan's Book*. But the young gentleman now knows Greek, and I hardly like to offer it to him. And yet I think I will.

Part I

EXTERNALS

I

PRELIMINARY

in which some words and titles are defined

IN spite of the great abundance and originality of English
Literature the most famous book in the language is not an
original work but a translation. It is what we call the BIBLE,
a name which is derived from Greek and properly means
Books. The Bible is in fact a collection of books translated
partly from Hebrew and partly from Greek. There have been
several English translations, some of which are quite recent,
but far the most widely circulated is the AUTHORISED VERSION
of 1611, described on its title-page as 'translated out of the
original tongues: and with the former translations diligently
compared and revised by His Majesty's special command.'

The Bible or collection of Books falls easily into three
divisions, the OLD TESTAMENT, the APOCRYPHA, the NEW
TESTAMENT. The Old Testament consists of the sacred books
of the Jews which were originally written in Hebrew. The
Apocrypha consists of other sacred books of the Jews written
originally partly in Hebrew and partly in Greek, and belonging
to a later period than the Old Testament. The New Testament
consists of the sacred books of the Christians originally written
in Greek.

All these books have been translated into many tongues,
and of these VERSIONS (as translations of Holy Scripture are
called) the three most celebrated are a Greek version of the
Old Testament, and a Latin and an English version of the
whole Bible. The first of these is the celebrated Greek version of the Old Testament, called the SEPTUAGINT because
seventy scholars of Alexandria are supposed to have made
it and SEPTUAGINTA is the Latin for seventy. The celebrated
Latin version of the Bible is the revision made by S. Jerome,
called the VULGATE because it is the popular one and has superseded all others; *vulgus* is the Latin for the common people,
and a book is *vulgate* when it has reached the people. The

11

celebrated English version is the AUTHORISED VERSION mentioned already, notable for its majestic style and for its wide diffusion across the world.

A volume which contains the Old and the New Testaments in Greek (with or without the Apocrypha) I should call a GREEK BIBLE. A volume which contained the Old Testament in Greek I should call a SEPTUAGINT. A volume which contained the New Testament in Greek I should call a GREEK TESTAMENT. It is with this last volume, the Greek New Testament, that the following pages have to do.

II

THE CONTENTS OF THE NEW TESTAMENT

twenty-seven items in all

A PRINTED Greek Testament commonly contains the same books as our English New Testament. It therefore comprises 27 different pieces. These may be sorted out as follows:—

I-IV	(*a*) *Four Gospels*, according to Matthew, Mark, Luke, John.
V	(*b*) *Acts of Apostles*, an historical account of the earliest years of the Church, by the same author as Luke's Gospel of which it is a continuation.
	(*c*) *Epistles* (i.e. Letters) assigned to Paul.
VI-IX	(i) Four great Epistles: to the Romans, Corinthians (2), Galatians.
X-XIII	(ii) Three Epistles and a personal letter, written during Paul's captivity in Rome: to the Ephesians, Philippians, Colossians, Philemon (some have thought that Paul did not write Ephesians).

12

XIV-XV (iii) Two Epistles to the Thessalonians: rather early compositions.

XVI-XVIII (iv) Three Pastoral Epistles: to Timothy (2), to Titus: rather late composition, possibly not by Paul.

XIX (v) The Epistle to the Hebrews, probably not by Paul. These fourteen items, forming the *corpus Paulinum*, are arranged more or less according to their length, the longest coming first. But Hebrews, though long, comes last as being of doubtful authorship.

XX-XXVI (*d*) *Seven Catholic* (or general) *Epistles*, called by the names of Apostles: of James, Peter (2), John (3), Jude.

XXVII (*e*) *The Revelation* (or Apocalypse) of John the Divine. (This in form is an Epistle, addressed to seven Churches in Asia Minor.)

The order in which the books occur is perhaps on the whole as satisfactory as any. But in many early copies the Catholic Epistles are put either before or after the Acts, no doubt because of their connection with the Apostles. They come immediately after the Acts in Westcott and Hort's Greek Testament first published in 1881. It is a pity in some ways that Jude was not put after II Peter with which it has a clear connection, and this would have brought the three Epistles of John next to the Revelation. The Gospels were perhaps bound in honour to be put first of all, yet this seems to make it difficult for ordinary people to realise that at least ten of the Epistles were written before any of the Gospels.

III

DATES

a section which should be historical but is not

IT is natural to ask: when was the New Testament written?
And the answer must be that none of the books are actually
dated. For ten Epistles of Paul we can be fairly certain of the
date within a very few years, while for the rest we can only
make rather precarious conjectures. The whole business is
fully dealt with in Hastings' *Dictionary of the Bible* in an
article on Chronology (New Testament) by C. H. Turner. This
article has become almost classical, and is not likely to be
much improved upon.

We should not be far wrong if we thought of I and II Thessalonians as having been written about A.D. 50; I and II
Corinthians and Romans about A.D. 55; Ephesians, Philippians, Colossians and Philemon about A.D. 60. In regard to
Galatians there is more of a question. Formerly it was
grouped with Corinthians and Romans and thought of as
probably preceding Romans by a year or two, but recently
there has been a wish to fit it in as the earliest of Paul's writings and assign it to a date as early as A.D. 48. In that case
it is the earliest extant Christian writing by several years.

Anyway what we learn of Paul from Acts and from the
Epistles themselves enables us to get them into a series in
which the order is highly probable and the date correct within
a very few years. With the four Gospels it is quite otherwise.
Reputable scholars have put the date of the Gospel according
to John as far on as A.D. 140, though this is now thought to
be impossibly late. On the other hand general considerations
seem to lead to the conclusion that the earliest Gospel is later
than any of Paul's ten Epistles mentioned above. If we need
to form some notion of the matter we might think of Mark as
written about A.D. 65, Matthew about A.D. 75, Luke about
A.D. 85, John about A.D. 95. This is at least easy to remember,
and quite probably near the truth. It almost certainly gives
the order of the composition of the Gospels, and that is a
very important point. Matthew and Luke are possibly not

14

separated by so much as ten years, and John may be as early as the later eighties.

This accounts for 14 of the 27 pieces. Of the remaining 13 the Acts, the Epistle to the Hebrews, and Revelation are long books. We have not much but common sense to guide us in the dating of them. Acts may be put about ten years after the Gospel according to Luke, perhaps more, perhaps less. Hebrews does not read like a work of Paul, whose style and method are well marked. It is less enthusiastic and has the character of a thesis. But it cannot be dated long after the death of Paul, which occurred in A.D. 64, if not before. The three so-called Pastoral Epistles to Timothy and Titus, if by Paul, come in the early sixties, but some have abandoned the Pauline authorship and have put them very much later because in them the Church seems to be so much more highly organised than in the other Pauline Epistles. The three Epistles of John belong to the same period as the Gospel that goes by his name. The Revelation, if by the same author, may be an early work, if only because it shows a rather imperfect knowledge of Greek. It is difficult to think that John wrote it, but it is also difficult to argue that he did not, though Dionysius of Alexandria did argue persuasively to that effect on grounds of style as early as A.D. 260. The Epistle of James belongs to a time when there was a controversy about Faith and Works, and might be as early as the Epistle to the Romans or before it. The First Epistle of Peter is influenced by Paul, and must be put late in Peter's life, say A.D. 60, that is if it is by Peter, and why should it not be? There is no knowing about the Epistle of Jude, but it must have been well established by the time the so-called Second Epistle of Peter was written, since it is there largely reproduced; and it is likely enough that the Second Epistle of Peter belongs to the early second century. It is the black sheep of the canonical books of the New Testament, and we are allowed to wish it away. Peter cannot have written it, whoever else.

It is disappointing to have to deal so much in mere possibilities and probabilities in the dating of the books of the New Testament. But it is all we can do. What emerges is that we shall not be far wrong if we assume for general purposes the following dates:

| Gal. | A.D. 48 (or ?55) |
| I Thess., II Thess. | A.D. 50 |

15

I Cor., II Cor., Romans	A.D. 55
Eph., Phil., Col., Philem.	A.D. 60
Mark	A.D. 65
Matt.	A.D. 75
Luke	A.D. 85
John, Acts	A.D. 95

The New Testament in fact belongs to the second half of the first century.

IV

AUTHORSHIP AND AUTHENTICITY

very briefly touched upon

IF I ascribe authenticity to a statement or a book I mean that it comes from the author or source from which it claims to come. Thus when I read on a notice at the door of the Home Office that the Princess Elizabeth had been delivered of a Prince, I did not doubt the truth of it because I could reckon it was authentic, that is to say that the notice had been put up by order of the Home Secretary and that he had the information from Buckingham Palace and that he had verified it. If then the Epistle to Philemon is authentic, it must have been written by Paul when he was in prison, because that is what it says (Philem. 1.9, 19), and this being more probable than any other theory of its origin, I call Philemon authentic. In this sense the Gospels according to Mark and Luke, the Acts, at least nine or ten Epistles of Paul and most of the Catholic Epistles are definitely authentic. The authenticity of the rest has been disputed, and in regard to Hebrews and II Peter must be disallowed. But speaking in general terms there is no doubt about the authenticity of the New Testament. It does very largely consist of writings by prominent Christians of the generation after the Crucifixion, and that is what it professes to consist of.

But I cannot be altogether certain of identifying the names belonging to some of the books. I am not sure if John in all the five cases where his name indicates an author is the

16

same John, nor whether he is John the son of Zebedee one of the Twelve, or another John, the aged divine of Ephesus, or a young disciple of the Lord outside the circle of the Twelve. I am not sure if Matthew whose name is connected with the first Gospel is the same as Levi, called from the receipt of custom to be one of the Twelve (Mark 2.14). I do not know who wrote the Epistle to the Hebrews or the Second Epistle of Peter. I do, however, know a great deal about Paul and Luke and I feel fairly certain that between them they wrote just about half the New Testament. And of the whole it may be said that the inclusion of any item in the CANON, or standard edition as we should call it, is in itself a strong indication of authenticity. The books reached a certain tone and elevation which belonged peculiarly to the Christian Church of the first century. No formal list of the contents was drawn up until the collection was pretty well complete. But the test of being frequently read in church had established some writings and discredited others so that in different parts of the Christian community the same books were found to be in use. There was no intention at first to create a canonical New Testament alongside the Old, but it emerged in practice and was then accepted in theory.

V

TRANSMISSION

the beginnings of a long business

THERE is another sense in which we may ask whether the Greek Testament is authentic. We may ask whether the Greek TEXT (that is, the words) which we now have would be actually word for word what the authors wrote. The answer to this question is easy. There are places in the Greek Testament where we strongly suspect that we have not got what the authors wrote word for word. There is CORRUPTION of the text in some places. Nevertheless our text is astonishingly near to a pure text, that is, to what the authors wrote, considering how long ago the books were written, and that copies of them were made by hand over a period of quite 1,400 years.

And what is more we have material in the form of numerous ancient copies which if studied rightly can improve the text a great deal and remedy its corruption. But how all this has come about entails beginning at the beginning. It is a somewhat complicated business and therefore we cannot be too simple at the start.

Let us begin then with an obvious truth. All the books that have ever been written are now either forgotten or remembered. And if they are remembered it is because they have been transmitted to the readers of the present day. And clearly if the books were written long ago the process of transmission must have been elaborate. And certainly that has been so with the Greek Testament. The history of its transmission is long and elaborate, it is also interesting, and even romantic. It has for its background the fact that once a book has been written down it is normally transmitted to posterity by copying. And up to the present there have only been two ways of copying effectively: (*a*) by handwriting, (*b*) by printing. I take printing first because it is the most familiar.

VI

PRINT AND PAPER

inseparable companions

THE most important characteristic of printing is that it can produce a great many copies of a book which will all be exactly alike. They may contain misprints and even more substantial faults, but they are all alike, whereas no two copies of a book of any considerable length will be exactly alike if they are written out by hand.

Printed copies, however, can be and often are made to vary on purpose. For example, Fielding's *Tom Jones* was first published in 1749. My own copy is of an edition published by Methuen in 1927. A Prefatory Note tells me that the text is that of the edition of 1762 corrected by the Third Edition of 1750. Precisely the text in my copy was presumably never printed before 1927. It varies inconsiderably from former editions, but it does vary. Nor is the text precisely

18

what it sets out to be, because it is marred by misprints, as almost all printed books are. On page 75 in my copy and in all copies of this edition the last word of line 37 is *why* when it should be *who* and the last word of line 39 is *vero* when it should be *very*. It is clear that in the course of making some correction the printer has interchanged the final letters of lines 37 and 39, a mistake not unlikely in a printed book, though very unlikely in a book written by hand. To put *who* for *why* and *vero* for *very* in this passage is a certain EMENDATION.

In some cases the emendation of a misprinted text is not so certain. On page 282 of my *Tom Jones* there occurs a Latin quotation *Non si male nunc, et olim sic erit* (If things are ill now, they will not therefore be so presently). But it seems to me that the last word *erit* (will be) should be *erat* (was), if it is to make sense in the context in which it stands. If I had other copies of *Tom Jones* by me I should look the passage up in them, and if any respectable edition gave *erat* I should correct my corrupt copy by this better one. If all the editions gave *erit* I should still alter my *erit* to *erat*, but I should call this a CONJECTURE and not an emendation. Which only shows how dangerous conjecture is because the Latin words as a matter of fact are from Horace's Odes (2.10.17), and *erit* is right, though it makes the quotation somewhat inappropriate.

The errors in a printed book are not always due to the printer. They may be due to the author's handwriting being difficult to read or to his manuscript being ill revised. Wordsworth's handwriting was notoriously difficult to read, and there are probably still errors in the printed copies of his works which come from the HOLOGRAPH, as the original manuscript in the author's own handwriting is often called. Actually Wordsworth hated the physical process of writing and dictated his more important works to his wife or sister without writing them down himself at all.

Generally speaking, however, misprints are easy to correct. And if we ask what is the purpose of correcting them the answer is twofold: first, to make sense where the misprint makes nonsense, but secondly, and very important, to present a pure text of the book as the author wrote it or intended to write it. He may have made faults in the grammar and syntax, he may have been slovenly, he may have been mistaken in matters of fact, his views may be absurd. All that is proper material for the editor and commentator. But a pure text is
19

one which disregards all that and aims only at giving what the author meant to give. And the purpose of correcting a work in manuscript is exactly the same. To correct the text of the Greek Testament would have for its object to present what Peter and Paul and Mark and the rest of them actually wrote down for their readers.

And now we have come to TEXTUAL CRITICISM. For as K. Lake says, 'The object of all textual criticism is to recover so far as possible the actual words written by the writer.' (*The Text of the New Testament*. K. Lake. Rivington. p. 1—an admirable little book.)

VII

PAPYRUS AND PARCHMENT

ancient rivals

A DOCUMENT of any sort written by hand is called a MANUSCRIPT and, until the invention of printing, books could only be multiplied and circulated and transmitted in manuscript copies. As a printed copy of the Greek Testament was not available till 1516, its preservation from the first century onwards clearly depended for a very long time on manuscripts. Of such manuscripts containing the Greek Testament or some not inconsiderable part of it about 4,000 are reckoned to be still in existence, and it is safe to say that no two of these are exactly alike. The errors of addition, omission, repetition, alteration, are much more frequent than in a printed copy, but they are often much more interesting too, because they are not the result of failing to manipulate a machine but are due to human factors such as absence of mind, misdirection of the eye, misplaced intelligence, personal predilection, and so forth. The study of them is most absorbing to those who have a taste for it, and such students become textual critics. What they are aiming at is to sort out these thousands of copies of the Greek Testament and try to discover the text that was in the authors' original manuscripts. You might think this was a hopeless task. In fact it is not. But before trying to learn how the textual critics set about their work, it will be as well to consider under

20

what circumstances these manuscripts of the Greek Testament came into existence and were preserved.

The apostles and evangelists who wrote the New Testament wrote it on papȳrus. In the first century this was almost universally used to write upon, as paper is now. PAPYRUS is originally the name of a plant, a tall reed, noticeable because the stem is not round but three-sided, and it has a handsome feathery head, which C. R. Gregory calls 'a large inverted tassel of grass-like hair' (C. R. Gregory: *Canon and Text of the New Testament*, p. 301). Specimens of it may often be seen in the temperate conservatories of botanical gardens, at Kew, for instance, or in the Physic Garden at Oxford. To make the sheets of the famous writing material out of it the pith was cut into long narrow strips. These were laid side by side, and then another layer at right angles to the first was put upon the top of it. The sheet thus formed was pressed and dried and smoothed, and the result was a very tolerable piece of writing-paper or papyrus. The sheets were commonly made up in what we should call quarto size (that is to say about twice the size of a page of this book) but there was nothing to prevent them being a good deal larger or, of course, as small as you liked.

The author may have written right across the page when he was composing his book, but in getting it up for distribution the text was written in columns side by side. The columns would be perhaps three inches wide and separated from each other by about half an inch or a little more. The sheets were combined into a volume by the very cumbrous device of gumming one sheet to the next so that the whole formed a continuous length of papyrus. It could be rolled up when not in use and would be kept not on a shelf but in a sort of tub provided for the purpose. It was, in fact, easily stored, but this was about the whole sum of its convenience. Unrolling it to read would be as awkward as looking at a map which has been rolled up, and the unrolling was not good for the papyrus. It was peculiarly tiresome if you wished to look at a particular passage, especially if it was in the latter part of the book. And when you had finished reading, the whole work had to be rolled back again to the beginning before it could be read again. For all these reasons it became very inconvenient to have a roll more than about thirty feet long. The so-called books of Thucydides or Plato's *Republic* are merely sections which amount to about as much as would fill

21

an ordinary roll or volume. It has been reckoned that Luke or Acts may normally have been written on a roll of about thirty-three feet, and these are the longest books of the New Testament.

In a well got-up volume the top and bottom would display ornamental knobs at the end of the roller to which the last sheet was attached, and the front end would be finished off with a piece of coloured material which acted as a kind of dust-cover. But even when so protected this papyrus is fragile stuff. It chips off at the sides and develops rough rectangular holes corresponding to the edges of the slender strips of which it is composed. It is also easily spoiled by damp, and that is the reason why very little of it has been found except in Egypt where the climate is favourable to its preservation. In Egypt a vast amount of it no doubt still lies buried in the sand. Our knowledge of papyrus and the resulting science of papyrology is still in its childhood. Until the second half of the eighteenth century no papyri had been seen for more than a thousand years: and only in this century has their recovery and examination been either extensive or methodical.

Because of its fragile character papyrus always had a rival in parchment which was available in large quantities from about 200 B.C. The centre of the trade was at Pergamum in Asia Minor, and the word parchment is a corruption of Pergamene. It is applied to any writing material that is made of skin, most commonly of lamb or calf or kid. The finer kinds are called vellum. The very finest kind is said to have been made from the skins of unborn lambs. Ordinarily the skin would have hair on one side which had to be rubbed away, and this side is somewhat rougher than the other. Both sides, however, make a smooth, nearly white sheet, very difficult to destroy by fire or water, and almost impossible to tear. It tends to develop round or oval holes in it, and it does not take the ink so well as papyrus, especially on the inner side. In course of time the writing is apt to get faint. It does not roll so well as papyrus, though volumes up to twenty feet long are practicable.

We know that the earliest Christians sometimes used parchment because Paul writes to Timothy (II Tim. 4.13), *the cloke that I left at Troas with Carpus, bring when thou comest, and the books, especially the parchments* (*membranae* is the word in the Greek); but the second Epistle of John was written on papyrus (*chartēs* is the word in the Greek, II John 12), and

22

generally speaking papyrus would have been used for the earliest copies of the New Testament books, until it was rather suddenly superseded by parchment about the beginning of the fourth century.

And in consequence of this change another very important change also took place. Books begin to appear in the form in which they are familiar to us, that is not as rolls but as leaf books, where one or more leaves are folded into a gathering or quire, and the quires are sewn together side by side on the inner margin so as to form a single book, which to distinguish it from the roll or volume is called a CODEX (plural *codices*). This is a tremendous improvement. To begin with it is possible to make much larger books with the consequence that the four Gospels, for example, could easily be bound up together, whereas at first they must have been in separate rolls. The whole Greek Testament could easily be contained in two volumes, or even one if the pages were large. Furthermore it made it quite easy to look up a particular passage, and this was of great service to the Christian Church. There is good reason in fact to believe that it was the Christians who did most to promote the use of leaf-books, for nearly all the early specimens that have survived contain Christian writings.

Publishers however are very conservative, and the codices kept for a long time the narrow columns of writing which were really appropriate to the roll. And no wonder, for these columns have a beautiful appearance when they are well laid out on a large sheet, as anyone can see by looking at those two great manuscripts of the Greek Testament which are in the British Museum.

VIII

THE EXTANT MANUSCRIPTS

a study in survival

THE number of copies of the Greek Testament which have been produced is very large indeed. There have been more than a thousand printed editions, some of which consist of a great number of copies. But ultimately of course these are all derived from manuscripts. The first printed Greek Testament to appear, that of 1516, was edited by Erasmus. He got hold of a rather interesting but not very good manuscript and after correcting it by a worse one sent it straight to the printer. He might have done much better if he had got hold of older, plainer, and more accurate manuscripts, and incidentally he might have read the proofs, and corrected them better, if the publisher Froben had not been in a hurry to forestall Cardinal Ximenes's magnificent edition then awaiting publication in Spain. In the end of course the whole business of producing a good Greek Testament in print depends upon what sort of manuscripts are available.

It is clear from what has already been said that parchment has a good chance of surviving and papyrus a poor chance. And as the use of papyrus preceded that of parchment the earliest copies and certainly all the original copies of the books of the New Testament have perished. But it is equally true that the early parchment copies have perished except where they were preserved accidentally or because of their splendid appearance. The result is that most of the surviving manuscripts are late manuscripts, written after the tenth century and for the most part after the twelfth century. Up to the end of the nineteenth century scarcely one hundred New Testament manuscripts were assigned to any century earlier than the tenth. Since then new discoveries, mostly of papyri, may have increased this number by fifty, of which ten are important.

Naturally enough the early manuscripts are nearly always the most interesting. They are also the most beautiful. The very early ones, down to the end of the sixth century, are called UNCIALS, of which the literal English would be Inchers, suggesting that the letters were an inch high, though in actual usage a manuscript is called Uncial if it is written entirely in capital letters, whatever their size. Since 1750 the manuscripts have all been numbered, but the chief Uncials are distinguished also by Latin, Greek or Hebrew capital letters. The number of an Uncial always begins with a nought (0). Thus the celebrated Greek and Latin manuscript of the Gospels and Acts at Cambridge, the Codex Bezae, is indicated by the letter D, and also, though much less often, by the number 05. Some of the Uncials are very fine books in silver letters on purple vellum. But far more beautiful really are the very plain, very well written, and very dignified texts of the fourth century, ℵ (Aleph, the first letter of the Hebrew alphabet) and

24

A, both in the British Museum, and B in the Vatican. They are grand enough to have titles too, *Sinaiticus, Alexandrinus, Vaticanus* respectively. They are of course the work of professional scribes, and they have been carefully corrected. The history of *Sinaiticus* in modern times is most romantic. A very good pamphlet about it can be bought at the British Museum for a shilling or two.

Until recently these were reckoned our oldest manuscripts, and as the original works had appeared about 250 years before, there had obviously been plenty of time for a good deal of error to creep in through successive copying, especially in the earlier years, for then the text was written on papyrus, and at first by amateur scribes, and it was handled and passed round by the early Christians, many of whom were by no means scholars or even habitual readers. It might be thought that all we could do was to get back to the text that prevailed at the beginning of the fourth century. But there are in fact means of getting behind the fourth century as we shall see.

After the sixth century the Uncial writing in capital letters began to degenerate into 'semi-uncial' and then into a running hand similar to that which we use ourselves. To distinguish them from the Uncials, manuscripts so written are called CURSIVES, or MINUSCULES. They are catalogued by ordinary Arabic numerals which run into thousands. The two which Erasmus used are numbered 1 and 2 respectively. Though none of them were written in the first eight centuries, some are of interest, and 33 (in Paris) has been called the 'Queen of the cursives'. Cursive manuscripts are rarely, if ever, really handsome, but some are quite nice to look at.

From time to time new manuscripts of importance come to light. An Uncial copy of the Gospels (W) with some notable features appeared in 1906 in Egypt. It is now at Detroit, U.S.A. And in 1931 the discovery of a number of papyri in leaf-book form included considerable portions of a book which had contained the Gospels and Acts, and almost the whole of another containing ten Epistles of St. Paul (not Philem., I Tim., II Tim., Tit.). These belong to the early third century and therefore go back 100 years before ℵ A and B. The papyri are numbered with a large 𝔓 of Gothic type followed by an index number. The two items just mentioned are 𝔓45 and 𝔓46. Very small, but more remarkable still in its own way is a fragment of a Codex (𝔓52) containing John 18.31-33 which is assigned to the early second century by its editor, Mr. C. H.

25

Roberts. This brings it within fifty years of the original manuscript.

In modern times too, a great many copies have been examined for the first time or re-examined with greater care. Photographic facsimiles and photostats have made the study of them much easier than it used to be. Several hundred manuscripts have been carefully COLLATED, as it is called, that is to say have been carefully compared with a standard text and the variations noted. Of course the variations, commonly called the READINGS, are very numerous in themselves, but they are in fact very few in proportion to the material. When in 1707 Dr. John Mill published his great Greek Testament with 30,000 variant readings—far more than had ever been got together before—men said that the text of the New Testament must be utterly insecure. It was the great scholar Bentley who pointed out that so far from rendering the text of scripture insecure the *fewness* of the variants showed its great security compared to any classical texts. There are *only* about a thousand places in the whole New Testament where the variant readings in the Greek make the smallest difference to the sense, and not fifty where a point of doctrine is in question.

But we have to cope with these thousand places not only to satisfy the intellectual urge to solve a problem, but because the Christians have the custom of expounding in great detail the words of Jesus or Paul or Peter, and it is important to try and find out for sure just what those words were when they were first set down. And the minor variations have their own importance too on palaeographical grounds, and how palaeography works and what it does must next engage our attention.

IX

PALAEOGRAPHY

a difficult art until you get used to it

PEOPLE who have the opportunity of seeing many works of art of a particular kind, as for example water-colour paintings, or china, or coins, come to have a feeling for them, and palaeographers are people who have come to have a feeling for old writing. Out of these feelings they create a slightly precarious science which enables them to date manuscripts and often to say where they were written. Most manuscripts of proper books (as opposed to bills and letters and legal documents) are not dated, but a certain number are, either by an explicit statement or by some allusion in the text. By noting the characteristics of dated manuscripts the palaeographers judge an undated one and can assign it to its century. Though there will be some mistakes and differences of opinion it is not so very difficult. Most of us who make a habit of looking round second-hand book shops can do the same with printed books ourselves. The palaeographers do it with manuscripts.

We have already taken it for granted that of two manuscripts the older one is almost always of greater importance, that is to say, is the one that helps us to get nearer to the author's original text. And the reason for this is obvious. It is that in the course of copying variations will always be occurring. If a manuscript (call it P) is copied, the copy will contain a number of variations, and if this copy (call it Q) is copied, the new copy (call it R) will contain the variations of Q and some more of its own. And if R is copied the copy (call it S) will contain the variations of both Q and R as well as its own. Even if some of the more obvious errors are corrected by the scribe, Q will still be a better manuscript than R or S, because it will vary less from the original, but it will not be such a good one as P. To discover then that Q and R and S are derived from P will be very useful, because it makes Q and R and S so relatively unimportant. We can usually put them on one side. So after dating the manuscripts provisionally the palaeographer's next business is to trace their derivation.

This derivation, or DESCENT of manuscripts, as it is usually called, is often quite easy to trace. If two manuscripts have the same series of variations either one is derived from the other or both have a common ancestor. A whole group of manuscripts may prove to have a common ancestor. They are then called a FAMILY. The cursives 13, 69, 124, 346, 543, 788, 826, 828, 983, 1689, 1709 form a family which would be referred to as *fam. 13*. They were all written in Southern Italy about the twelfth century. The first four were copied from the same original. The common ancestor of a family may or may not be extant. If it is extant, we can usually afford to neglect its descendants. If it is not, we can take the best of its descendants, which will probably be the oldest of them.

27

There are however exceptions to this. If a tenth-century manuscript for example happens to have been copied from a fourth-century manuscript it should be superior to an eighth-century manuscript copied from a sixth-century manuscript. An interesting illustration of this is to be found in the importance of the manuscript Θ (thēta). It is a dirty little book (now, or at any rate until recently, at Tiflis), written in the ninth century in an execrable hand by a man who did not know Greek and hardly knew the Greek alphabet. Contrary to the usual practice he had got hold of an old and probably neglected manuscript from which to make his copy. He made frightful mistakes, so frightful that they are easily detected. But he did not try to understand his text, much less to improve it. His evidence therefore is most valuable in spite of himself.

But examples of such superiority are not frequent in connection with Greek Testament manuscripts. There was a feeling that a recent copy would be a better one, though in actual fact the precise opposite is almost completely true. But as this truth was not realised, what with copying and copying and re-copying and injudicious correcting, the record through the centuries is a continuous record of making improvements for the *worse*.

So generally speaking the oldest manuscripts are the best. And information as to the descent of a manuscript which can be obtained from dating is reinforced and sometimes superseded by the possibility of telling which of two manuscripts has been copied from the other merely by the kind of variations between them. One can usually do that even with two schoolboy exercises one of which is derived wholly or in part from the other. It is easy to tell who has cribbed. There are some kinds of error which can only arise directly out of the process of copying.

The ideal result of all this palaeography would be to discover among our very numerous manuscripts of the Greek Testament one which was the ancestor of all the rest. But this is not the actual result. What we discover is several ancestors giving as many types of text, perhaps four or five main types, which point to revision of the text at definite stages, and rather less certainly to very early ancestors belonging to different important Christian centres such as Antioch, Alexandria, Caesarea and Rome. But it must not be inferred from this that the Churches in these places, however venerable, ever possessed what was regarded as an official copy of the New Testament. What is true is that in each centre the congregations would get used to hearing the Scripture read out in a particular wording and when new rolls or books were written out for use in Church they would be ASSIMILATED to the local text. This local text moreover would be found to have some special insertion or variant reading of its own which was of interest to other churches, and it would be borrowed and inserted in manuscripts of a different type and ancestry, and thus CONTAMINATION would occur, and in fact it has occurred very extensively. From time to time some pope or bishop of a scholarly turn of mind would order an overhaul of the text, but we cannot say that there was any single tremendous overhaul of the Greek text of the same kind as there was of the Latin Bible when Jerome produced the Vulgate at the end of the fourth century. Origen however did a great deal of work on the text of the Greek Bible in the first half of the third century. But no standard text emerged, and the distinctive types of text remain recognisable, whatever their explanation.

X

VERSIONS AND QUOTATIONS

a glimpse behind the scenes

THE study of the manuscripts of the Greek New Testament settles a good deal, but it leaves a good deal unsettled too. It does not lead us back to any one earliest form of the text. It makes it appear likely that the original writings were very soon corrupted and then corrected independently in different parts of the world, and that the varying types of the text which thus emerged were thereafter constantly contaminated by one another. So we need all the further help we can get, and, as it happens, we can go behind the manuscripts in two ways, first of all, by examining the Versions, secondly, by seeing in what form the text is quoted by the FATHERS, that is, by the early Christian writers outside the New Testament.

Naturally enough the books of the New Testament were translated into foreign languages before long. By the middle of the second century there were several Versions of which the Latin, the Syriac, and the Egyptian circulated most widely. The importance of these Versions is that they must have been made from Greek manuscripts older than any we now possess except possibly one or two on papyrus. And fortunately the early Christians made extremely literal versions and it is not too difficult to see the Greek text that lies behind them. This is not as good as having a very early manuscript, but it serves the same purpose to a considerable extent. Picture then an early Christian, perhaps not much of a scholar, sitting down to translate a book of the Greek Testament into Latin. He gets hold of a Greek manuscript. We hope it is a good one, at any rate it is older than any we have now. He then proceeds to turn it into Latin as closely as he can without much regard for style and (fortunately) with no regard at all for underlying meanings. He sticks to his last and finishes his job. And what has happened to his book? It is lost. We have not any manuscripts of the Versions left which are very old. Like the Greek they have suffered from corruption and revision and contamination. There are a vast number of manuscript copies of the Latin version, perhaps 8,000, but hardly two dozen of them go behind the Vulgate text and not one perhaps was actually written before the Vulgate appeared. Nevertheless we can still see plainly enough that the old Latin version was taken from a Greek text that was not of the type of א and B, but of the same type as D, and this allows a greater antiquity to be assigned to the text of D than D itself would show. The testimony of the Versions is not easy to interpret, but it can supplement substantially what the Greek manuscripts themselves have to tell.

And another secondary source of information is provided by the quotations from the New Testament which we find in the Fathers. The Fathers had frequent occasion, of course, to expound the Scriptures or quote them in support of an argument. And very often it was necessary to quote them correctly, otherwise their arguments and expositions would come to nothing. If then under these conditions the Patristic quotations, as they are called, coming from a particular author consistently present one type of text, it raises a strong presumption that that type of text was used in that part of the world in which this author lived. Here lies the best chance we have of saying where the different types of text originated. The classic case is that of Origen. He began his Commentary on St. John about A.D. 231 in Alexandria. Before he had finished it he had moved to Caesarea. In the earlier book of the Commentary his New Testament quotations are from one type of text, in the later books from another. If we could make his places of residence correspond with his types of text we should call these different texts Alexandrian and Caesarean with confidence. But in fact the correspondence is by no means made out for certain. The evidence of the Patristic quotations is rather precarious. And it is easy to guess that in the works of the Fathers as we have them the scribes have often adjusted the quotations to the text with which they are familiar themselves. This makes it more precarious still. All the same the Versions and the Fathers can be of much service in the study of the Greek Testament to scholars who have the right equipment, and it is proper for everybody to know why and how the Greek text can be established by the use of translations and of books that are themselves no part of the New Testament.

The whole result of this palaeographical approach to the Greek Testament is inconclusive. There are several types of text, and this suggests early revisions and recensions. But even the early papyri 𝔓45 and 𝔓46 are considerably contaminated and do not point to any one type as more authentic than the rest. It used to be thought that an agreement between ℵ and B was almost bound to be accepted, but this is not now so certain. These two great manuscripts represent a most carefully preserved and widely accepted text, but D and W and fam. 13 and the old Latin and others too which have variations from them of quite a drastic kind no doubt preserve the true tradition in some places. It is not impossible that an isolated reading in some comparatively humble manuscript may give what the apostle or evangelist wrote. We must still be prepared to consider any particular passage on its merits, and not infrequently to refuse to decide between two different readings, as in practice the editors of the Revised Version did by putting alternatives in their margin. Palaeography shows that ℵ and B must have great weight attached to them, but it also shows that they are far from infallible.

But in any case, in spite of variant readings and types of text, the Greek Testament may be regarded as securing to us in all essentials what the first Christian writers wrote. The Christians to-day may read and quote their New Testament

31

as being truly a record and a voice from their earliest origins, but in some places they must quote it with just a little, a very little, reserve.

XI

ON BUYING A GREEK TESTAMENT

a question of getting your money's worth

WITH no more than a little Greek it is perhaps not possible to go much further with the Greek text of the New Testament. But if you know no more than how to spell out the alphabet, even that will make it worth your while to have a Greek Testament. You may find out a number of interesting things, as for example that Jerusalem has two names in Greek, that Jesus and Joshua are the same name, that pneumatic and spiritual really mean the same thing, that character is both an English word and a Greek word; and, if you like, you can go on and teach yourself a lot more than that, and things of greater importance too. So have a Greek Testament.

Presumably you will have a printed copy. It may cost you only ninepence off a barrow and yet be quite a nice one. You might occasionally be able to buy the most superior kind, the Complutensian Polyglot by name, for £500 or thereabouts, but it might not be the most useful for you to have, even if you could get it. What you will look for ordinarily will be what you look for in every book, a good text, good type, good binding. And if you are interested in the variant readings you will look for a good APPARATUS CRITICUS at the bottom of each page. This apparatus will tell you by a system of symbols already partly explained above which manuscripts have some particular reading. It may be a brief or a full apparatus, that is to say it may give variants at many places or at few; it may give the readings at any one place from many manuscripts or from few.

For example, Matt. 17.21 in the Authorised Version runs, *Howbeit this kind goeth not out but by prayer and fasting.* In the Revised Version it is omitted altogether. You look in an apparatus criticus to see why. In Souter's Oxford edition of the Greek Testament with a brief apparatus (1910) it tells you that the verse is omitted by ℵ B 33, that is to say by the two great Uncials and 'the Queen of the cursives', a sufficient condemnation of the verse. In S. C. E. Legg's very full apparatus (a wonderful piece of work) it tells you more. It tells you that the verse is omitted in ℵ B Θ 33, 892, 1604. This makes you think amongst other things that 892 and 1604 may be rather good cursives.

It is quite amusing, to say the least of it, to have some sort of apparatus criticus at the bottom of the page, and Souter's edition which gives the text of which the Revised Version is a translation is probably the most useful. An improved edition was brought out in 1947, but the older ones are still quite adequate for most purposes. It is more useful than Westcott and Hort (often shortened in writing to WH) which was thought very scientific for many years after its first appearance in 1881. But WH has no proper apparatus, it gives the books in an unusual order, and it is badly printed. Print counts for a good deal in Greek because it is such a beautiful script. Some of the common editions of the nineteenth century are very well printed, but all before Westcott and Hort gave the Received or Byzantine Text, which is roughly what our Authorised Version is taken from. It is what they call a long text and admits a good many clauses and verses (as for instance Matt. 17.21 dealt with above) which are not likely to have been in the author's text. It represents the final form which the New Testament assumed first in Constantinople and then throughout Eastern Christendom. It is the historic Greek Testament, even if it is not the most authentic.

Some of the old editions are always worth having when they come to hand. There had been close on four hundred of them by the end of the eighteenth century, of which I shall briefly mention five.

In 1707 Dr. John Mill published at the Clarendon Press at Oxford the great folio edition of his *Novum Testamentum Graece* with a very long introduction in Latin and an apparatus criticus far more complete than anything that went before, the result of thirty years of unremitting labour. This is a very fine book and not difficult to get for about 30s. The text is printed in a large flowery type and the lay-out of the page is dignified. In 1710 Kuster brought out a pirated edition of Mill at Amsterdam. This is a much less noble volume and should not be accepted as a substitute, though I once bought one for 4s. 6d., and it is certainly easier to use.

The claim of Mill's edition is aesthetic and historical. Of a very different kind is the edition published in 1729 in London anonymously. It was in fact by Daniel Mace, an obscure Presbyterian minister at Newbury. Mace did all the right things. First of all he did not print the Received Text, but a Text which in a number of places he had himself 'corrected from the Authority of the most Authentic Manuscripts', so the title-page informs us. Secondly, he printed it in a very plain type without any accents or fancy ornaments or unnecessary capital letters. Thirdly, he re-translated the whole New Testament and put the Greek and the English side by side. Fourthly, he appended some notes on the manuscript readings at the end of each book. Fifthly, he made a 'copious Alphabetical Index' to the whole. A modern scholar could not have attempted more, but no one took any notice of Daniel Mace or his book. He was before his time by more than 150 years. In 1934 I bought a moderately good copy for 10s. 6d.

Very different from these two modest volumes are the great Polyglots, so called because they give the Bible text in many languages. The London Polyglot, compiled during the Commonwealth, under the direction of Brian Walton, afterwards Bishop of Chester, is not the most sumptuous of these, but its six volumes make a handsome show, and it displays as many as nine languages. A sound copy will cost something like £50. It is still very useful to scholars. To its Greek text it appends variants from Codex Alexandrinus which had come to England about twenty years before. The Codex is indicated by the letter A, which is the origin of distinguishing manuscripts by the letters of the alphabet. But the systematic use of letters in this way was first made by J. J. Wettstein whose edition of 1751 deserves notice because it contains a great collection of parallel and illustrative passages from the pagan classics which still provides the commentators with useful material.

And finally there is the Complutensian Polyglot, an edition of the Bible in six great volumes and in three languages, produced at Alcalá near Madrid by the great Cardinal Ximenes in 1522. The Latin name for Alcalá is Complutum, and it is a piece of elegance to call this edition 'the Complutum'. Although Erasmus's Greek Testament appeared in 1516, the Complutensian edition was really the first to be printed. The New Testament was ready in 1514. A special Greek type based on Uncial script was designed and founded for it. The Old Testament is given in Hebrew, Greek and Latin, and the first five books in Aramaic also. The New Testament is in Greek and Latin. There are extensive introductions and appendices. The title-page and tail-piece (the COLOPHON) are fine. The Cardinal had 600 copies printed, and they were sold at about one-twelfth of the cost price. About a hundred copies, some very imperfect, are still known to exist. A good one is a beautiful thing. I have what was the Aldenham House copy, once in the convent of the Austin Friars at Antwerp. It is in a good vellum binding and contains the rare introduction to the Pauline Epistles and is perfect, a nice thing for an ageing clergyman to have by him.

Part II

INTERPRETATION

XII

THE GREEK LANGUAGE

a not wholly imperfect instrument

IN the Greek Testament we have the text of some ancient writings which we believe to have come down to us in the original language and pretty well exactly as the authors wrote them. Our business with them of course is to read and interpret them. Now interpretation comprises two things, because there is a clear difference between what a piece of writing says and what it means. Thus when I read Shakespeare's *Hamlet* I may have to ask myself in a number of places what Shakespeare was intending to say. He may have been obscure or I may have been dense, or some of the words may have altered their meaning since his day or I may never have met them before. I must remedy all this and make out the sense. But what the effect upon me will be when I have made it out is quite another thing. The feelings it arouses, the pleasure it gives, the questions it raises in my mind, and what (if anything) it inspires me to do, is not the sense of *Hamlet,* but the meaning. It is what the play can effect as a work of art.

And similarly in approaching the New Testament there is the question of what it says and the further, doubtless bigger, question of what it means. Both are matters of interpretation, but the first is concerned with language, and the second with ideas. It is logical to take language first.

The New Testament was written in Greek, and Greek is a most remarkable language, and to say what makes it remarkable is not so very difficult. To begin with much of the world's literature which is indisputably of the first rank is in the Greek language. This would include the two epics of Homer, the histories of Herodotus and Thucydides, the speeches of Demosthenes, the dialogues of Plato, and some hundreds of great tragedies of which only about thirty have survived. And to these mighty works of art we must add the extensive writings of Aristotle on science and philosophy, and much the greater part of Christian theology in the first five centuries. Greek

39

literature is almost as remarkable for its quantity as for its quality.

It is also a language which has undergone remarkably little change in the course of some twenty-three centuries. Latin has changed into French and Italian and Spanish, all three of which differ from it considerably, but the Greek of to-day is substantially the Greek of ancient Athens, and a classical scholar of only fair attainments in Greek will have little difficulty in reading a Greek newspaper. It is true that this is partly because in the last fifty years there has been a movement for making modern Greek more like the ancient; it has been a successful movement, whereas a similar movement to make the Romance languages more like Latin would be futile.

Again the language is remarkably free from foreign elements. The old Athenians for all their powers of mind and intellectual curiosity had almost no interest in foreign languages. They certainly did not think them of any educational value. It was they who invented the word barbarian, and it meant, at any rate to start with, a person who did not speak Greek. There are Phrygian and Celtic words in Greek to be sure, and words from other sources too. But generally speaking it is very pure, peculiarly unlike English in that respect. In English many of the best effects are obtained by judiciously mixing the Saxon words with the Latin importations (e.g. 'that we may *perfectly love* thee, and *worthily magnify* thy holy name'). In Greek this is hardly possible at all; on the other hand Greek had in its own uniform nature a great power of coining and compounding words to express a new refinement of thought or meaning. It has in consequence a very large vocabulary. Its grammar is slightly complicated, but suffered a gradual simplification. The construction of the sentences admits a great deal of variety without becoming cumbrous; and even when it is cumbrous, as often in Thucydides and not infrequently in the Apostle Paul, it can be uncommonly interesting, and there is a certain informality about it which makes it much less heavy-handed than Latin or German. It is vivid in narrative, and can be very ornamental without being grandiose in verse.

In our own time Greek has become remarkable in a new way. Almost all the fresh words that have been introduced into English to meet the needs of science are in fact Greek words. All the words that end in -ism, -ology and -ic, nearly every name in chemistry, many in sport, many in trade, thousands and thousands in all, are very closely derived from Greek. And this has happened just when Greek studies have shrunk excessively, so that in most cases the new words have to be learnt by rote instead of with the understanding, a very great pity. How many know why an acrostic, a philatelist, or even an economist is so called?

The origin of Greek is obscure, but so is the origin of all languages. It came into Greece from the North. Its cradle, if it can be said to have had one, would be in the neighbourhood of Albania. The geographical peculiarities of Greece, which is cut up by its many mountain ranges into numerous small plains and vales, gave rise to a number of dialects. One of these prevailed in Athens and as found there it is called Attic. It is the classical Greek which is studied in schools and colleges. In a somewhat different form the same dialect crossed the Aegean sea and was to be heard on the coast of Asia Minor round about Miletus, and in some of the intervening islands. As spoken in Asia Minor it was called Ionic, and the district was called Ionia. And it was in Ionia that the first literary movement occurred which gave rise to the classic Greek literature. The movement died down in Ionia, but culminated in an unparalleled achievement in Athens. It was as though the English spoken in America was brought back as a literary medium to England and there blossomed into an output of literature so far unequalled in this island, a thing in point of fact which well might happen. And if it should happen, the parallel would be closer from the circumstance that England and America would still have Shakespeare, as all Greece in the fifth century B.C. had Homer, whose works were by then four or five centuries old.

This blossoming of Attic literature coincided almost exactly with the fifth century, and then collapsed rather quickly. The centuries before and after were centuries of science rather than of literature. About 330 B.C. however the spoken language, hitherto confined more or less to Greece, the Aegean, southern Italy and some of the seaports further afield, spread over Palestine, Mesopotamia, and all the Middle East as one consequence of the victories of Alexander the Great, and in the city of Alexandria, which he founded in 331 B.C., a new and intense Greek learning was fostered and continued for some centuries. A new literature arose, and as a result of it, at the time when the New Testament was being written, two

41

ways of writing Greek were current, the way of reviving the old classical style which was finally achieved delightfully by Lucian in the second century A.D., and the other way of giving the spoken language a literary turn, which was practised by Plutarch who flourished about the year A.D. 100 and may be regarded as a junior contemporary of the New Testament writers.

Lucian would be called a writer of the neo-Attic school. Plutarch wrote in the KOINÉ, and that is also the language of the New Testament. Koiné means the common language. It is what people had come to speak and use as a general means of communication throughout the Roman Empire east of Rome and even in Rome itself. Employed in written works it was not necessarily very simple or colloquial, but it used the vocabulary of the spoken language and had some of its simplicity and some of its slovenliness. It also was capable of retaining the vividness and directness of speech, and this is seen nowhere more clearly than in the Gospels.

XIII

WORDS

about 5,420 different ones

I N reading the first thing, as we all remember, is to learn the alphabet. And in Greek this is easy. The letters have never been wholly disused, since they were gradually shaped into the form in which we know them, first as Uncials, and then some centuries later as a cursive script, composed of what we tend to call the ordinary letters because they are much like the Greek type in modern printed books.

But passing beyond the baby stage of the alphabet, the interpretation of a writing depends first and foremost on knowing what the words mean, or rather what they meant at the time when they were written down. Now the meaning of words is learnt by observing when they are used. It is at meal times for example that a child learns what the word *plate* means. Consequently in an ancient writing the meaning of the words will only be easy to ascertain if many writings in the same language and of the same time survive. And as a great deal of ancient Greek literature has survived, the meaning of all the ordinary Greek words is clear, at any rate for the fifth and fourth centuries B.C. For the first century A.D. it is not quite so clear because far less literature of that period exists. Still, most ordinary words do not alter their meaning much, and as the Greek Testament, like any book that is not highly technical, consists mostly of ordinary words it is generally speaking easy to know what the words in it mean.

There are however some circumstances which tend to obscure the meaning. First, words may have come to have some particular meaning which it is not easy to trace. But here the papyri come to our rescue. For the papyri consist to a comparatively small extent of literary works. They are largely the contents of ancient waste-paper baskets and rubbish bins, and this is no bad thing from our point of view. We find letters and papers of a purely temporary importance, but they tell us just what the words meant at the time of writing, and as many of the papyri can be dated quite accurately, they serve to interpret the temporary and changing and informal elements of the language. This has thrown a great deal of light on the Koiné. It has shown for example that the refinements which Bishop Westcott saw in the Greek of St. John's Gospel were often his own invention, for they are refinements of which Attic Greek of the fifth century was capable, but they had altogether disappeared from the Koiné. The papyri also enable us to give a precise meaning to many of the words.

Two examples of this will serve. In Mark 12.1 : Matt. 21.33 we read that *A certain man planted a vineyard and set an hedge about it, and digged a place for the winefat, and built a tower*. The old commentaries told you that the tower was a watch-tower, but we now know that the Greek word here, though it does ordinarily mean a tower, was probably also used for a set of farm buildings. This is just what the context requires. Again there is a famous Greek word *Parousia* of which the ordinary meaning is Presence. But it is used more often than not in the New Testament, where it occurs 24 times, of what we call the Second Coming of Christ; and it lights up the meaning a good deal when we find that it had come to be the proper word for what we call ' a royal visit '.

Secondly, although the words in the Greek Testament are mostly ordinary words, there are some which are very rare or even unique. The interpretation of such words depends on examining the context and on common sense, the same two resources which a schoolboy employs or ought to employ when he attempts to translate an 'unseen' passage from a foreign language. But since the New Testament has been very intensively studied we need not make it out like schoolboys; we can take a short cut and read up what different scholars have said and choose what seems the best sense.

Two examples will suffice again. In Mark 14.3: John 12.3 we read of an alabaster box of ointment of *spikenard*. The margin of the Revised Version tells us that the Greek for spikenard is *pistic nard*. Now this word pistic occurs nowhere else, so we may think what we like about its meaning. The Revised Version suggests that it is a local name for some particular kind of nard or balsam, or that it means *genuine*, or that it means *liquid*. You may take your choice. Secondly, in Phil. 2.6 Paul speaks of *Christ Jesus, who being in the form of God, thought it not robbery to be equal with God*. This really does not make much sense, and the word translated *robbery* occurs nowhere else in the Greek Bible, and only once in pagan literature, though that one place significantly is in Paul's contemporary Plutarch. The early translators put down *robbery* because there is a very similar word of the same derivation but much commoner which does mean robbery or snatching. But really we must guess the meaning in this passage from the context. And Bishop Lightfoot is probably right (he usually is) when he says it means that Christ 'did not look upon equality with God as a prize which must not slip from his grasp (but he emptied himself' etc.) (Lightfoot: *Philippians*, p. 111).

A third circumstance of some difficulty in interpreting the words arises from the fact that quite a number of them came to have a specialised meaning in the Christian community. We have only to read St. Paul's Epistles to see how much interested he was in the virtues and vices. He has several lists of both of them (see e.g. Gal. 5.19-21a, 22-23). Now this is characteristic of his age. The great celebrity which Plutarch has enjoyed is due to his studies of character in *The Parallel Lives* and in his work on *Morals*. He always exhibits the greatest interest in men's qualities, whether good or bad, and analyses them very closely. Paul has the same tendency.

Here again two examples will suffice; they are both quite familiar. One is the virtue of *humility*. It is a commonplace that this, which was regarded as a weakness, if not a vice, in the Greek and Roman pagan world, was elevated into a virtue by the Christians almost at once. They gloried in One *who, when he was reviled, reviled not again; when he suffered, he threatened not* (I Pet. 2.23). Humility was inherent in the religion of the Cross, while the pagans only laughed at the Cross and at humility too. The word appears in new contexts in the Greek Testament. And secondly, there is the celebrated word *Agapé*, Love. There is not the slightest doubt what this word means, because the corresponding verb and adjective for 'to love' and 'beloved' are very common in Greek. But this particular noun only occurs a few times in the Septuagint, and never in pagan authors, but something like 120 times in the Greek Testament. We shall therefore miss the meaning if we think of it as an ordinary word. It is one of *the* words in the earliest Church. It strikes a Christian note wherever it is heard.

There are a few words which scarcely form a class by themselves, but are nevertheless rather puzzling, because they are apparently due to ignorance of the language on the part of the writer. An example is in I Pet. 5.10: *The God of all grace . . . make you perfect, stablish, strengthen, settle you.* The word for *strengthen* occurs nowhere else in Greek literature. It is derived quite normally from the common word for strength, but it did not happen to exist. It is as though an English writer were to put down 'firmen'. That would be very odd, but anyone would guess that he meant 'strengthen'. Again in Heb. 11.37 where it says of the martyrs *that they were sawn asunder, they were tempted, they were slain with the sword,* when it says 'tempted' the author may be trying to say that they were 'pierced', but if so he has got it wrong.

So much for words. It is clear that the vocabulary of the Greek Testament contains meanings and associations which are lost in a translation, though the general sense of them is plain enough. But it is important not to generalise too much. The gospels have a surprisingly small vocabulary. Mark has only about 1,330 distinct words, including proper names. About 80 of these do not occur in any other book of the Greek Testament. The whole Greek Testament contains above 5,400 different words, and of these Paul contributes a great number. His Epistles are extremely hard to make out for the most part, mainly because of the way he strings the words together and because of his own peculiarities of style.

XIV

STYLE

a rather elusive thing

THERE cannot be any question of style in the use of a single word, because there is nothing to be done with it by itself except to use it in its proper form. But as soon as even two or three quite short sentences are put together, composition begins and problems of style at once arise. The writer must keep on deciding whether to use this word or that, whether to put the words in this order or some other order, whether to say some particular thing or leave it out. These decisions create the author's style. They may become very complicated, and to write about style at all is in consequence very difficult, so we will keep to the simplest elements of it. Assuming that a writer has something to say, he may do it stylishly or not stylishly, according as he solves these problems of choice correctly or otherwise. What you do or do not say, in what words you choose to have your say, and in what order you put your words, that is what good or bad style turns upon.

Of course some writers take a great deal more pains about their style than others, though they do not necessarily obtain a better result. Walter Pater was a very painstaking stylist, Walter Scott reeled off page after page day after day, but many would say that Scott had a better style than Pater. And there is always a personal factor in style. A man writes well if he has a style to suit him. The poet Gerard Manley Hopkins is a good example of this. His style suits him, but in his imitators it is often mere mannerism.

Style moreover does not depend wholly on the author's taste and judgment. It depends to a considerable degree on the character of the language he is writing in. He can only do what the language will let him do. Good style in French and English alike has the qualities of lucidity, interest, and ornament, but French is a more lucid language than English, while English is the more ornamental.

Now the Koiné is certainly capable of style. It is easy to see the difference in style between St. John's Gospel and the

more elaborate passages of St. Paul's Epistles, between John
1.1-14 and Eph. 1.1-14 for example, even in translation. But
the question is whether either John or Paul writes in *good*
style. And one may fairly ask if it is possible to judge whether
the style is good without some more or less intimate knowledge
of Greek.

Well, it is possible to some extent, because the Authorised
Version is really rather a literal translation of the Greek. It
has not the appearance of being so. It has all the appearance of coming from the common stock and idiom of the
English language as we use and speak it. There is hardly
a colloquial turn in English which is not somewhere in the
English Bible, except what in modern times has come from
America. This is partly because Tyndale and other early
translators had a great feeling for the language, and introduced
the colloquial with great effect, just as Mr. Winston Churchill
does. But it is also because we have borrowed so much from
the English Bible and have made it part and parcel of our
ordinary speech. It is not that the Bible drew on the ordinary
speech so much as that the ordinary speech has drawn on the
Bible. A good deal of the English translation of the Greek
Testament must have seemed very bald when it first appeared,
and in some places real dog English. *The God of glory*
(Acts 7.2) for example would be a very odd expression in
English, if we were not used to it. It is a literal translation
of the Greek, which itself translates the Hebrew idiom. But
it offers no difficulty now. The idiom has grown familiar,
and we find how familiar when we read in the Revised Version
at Phil. 3.21 a similar expression, namely *the body of our
humiliation*, and in the version of the Book of Common Prayer
of 1928 at the same place *the body of our low estate*. Neither
of these phrases really means much in English, and Tyndale
and the Authorised Version did not venture to be literal.
They put *vile bodies* which is plain enough but a paraphrase.
But by now we have become used to this Hebraism in English
from finding it in the Bible. *God of glory* was hardly English
at first, but it is so now. There is some brilliant paraphrasing
in the Authorised Version. But on the whole it is literal, and
you get from it more idea of the style of the Greek without
knowing Greek than is usual when you can only read a book
in translation.

I say that on the whole the Authorised Version is literal.
But it is very judicious about this. The Revised Version is in

many places more literal, the Revisers would have said in the interests of exact scholarship, but I am afraid we must say that they often fall into pedantry. The example I have just quoted illustrates this. *The body of our humiliation* is not an improvement on *vile bodies*, at any rate from the point of view of sense or style. There are plenty of other instances of the same sort of thing. In Mark 1.14 the Revised Version says that John the Baptist was *delivered up*; the Authorised Version had said much more naturally and with better sense *was put in prison*. In Mark. 3.6 the Revised Version says *the Pharisees went out and straightway with the Herodians took counsel*, and this represents the order of the Greek words, but it is dead contrary to the English idiom which the Authorised Version employs: *the Pharisees went forth and straightway took counsel with the Herodians*. In Mark 5.30 we read in the Revised Version *Jesus perceiving in himself that the power proceeding from him had gone forth*, a very ill-sounding phrase where the Authorised Version had some very simple and eloquent words which have almost passed into a proverb: *Jesus knowing in himself that virtue had gone out of him*. The Revisers were certainly better informed Greek scholars than those who produced the Authorised Version but they were much worse translators. A new company of scholars have recently been got together to produce a new translation. They are very distinguished and we may expect much of them.

It is clear that the language of the Greek Testament is eminently capable of telling a straightforward story. The miracles in Mark are admirably told, and Matthew and Luke did not make much attempt to improve upon him. John can do the same thing too, as in the Healing of the Nobleman's son (John 4.46-53). Luke puts the story of St. Paul's Conversion into Acts three times (Acts 9.3ff., 22.6ff., 26.12ff.) and it is a very well told tale. But we have to remember that all these stories had been told over and over again by word of mouth among the Christians before anyone tried to put them down on paper, and in the process they have gained a quality and style of their own. St. Paul in his own writings sometimes tells a story too. But he dramatises himself, and is hardly so successful. Almost all his most characteristic effects are got by accumulation, as in II Cor. 11.24-28 where he makes a list of his labours on behalf of the Gospel, twenty-three kinds of them; or a list of twenty-nine experiences by which he approved himself as a minister of God (II Cor. 6.4-10); or by piling up a tremendous long sentence, as at the beginning of Ephesians or Colossians; or by mere accumulation of genitives—*the light of the knowledge of the glory of God in the face of Jesus Christ* (II Cor. 4.6). Paul is not an elegant writer, but his struggles with the language match the powerful energy of the emerging thoughts which he is determined to express if he can. When he indulges in fine writing he is apt to overreach himself, as he does in the rather artificial praise of Charity in I Cor. 13, where the English version has toned him down considerably.

Of conscious literary style there is something in I Peter, possibly because the author is very much under the influence of Paul and tries to imitate him, but by nature he is a better writer than Paul. There is still more style in Hebrews, because the writer is expounding a thesis and has something to prove; and there is a peculiar air of it in Luke, partly because he is so fond of a well told story. Robert Bridges called the story of the Prodigal Son (Luke 15.11-32) 'an absolutely faultless piece of work' (*Collected Essays* XVII ad fin.). But there is another strain in Luke, especially in Acts. He seems to have been the first of the New Testament authors to suspect that he was writing Holy Scripture. He regards himself as a historian, but he has in mind the historical books of the Old Testament rather than Thucydides or Polybius. And he uses so many words out of the Septuagint that he must have been doing it consciously. Nevertheless he moves with ease in the Greek-speaking world, and Acts is in fact one of the chief secondary sources of information about the provincial administration of the Roman Empire. And he begins his Gospel with an elaborate preface in the classical style (Luke 1.1-4). It happens however not to be a very successful piece of writing, and he is more successful as soon as he begins to have the Jewish scriptures in view. As we read Paul we see a Jewish religion being brought to a Greek world, but Luke, though less of a missionary, did more in his own way than Paul to harmonise the sacred literature of the Jews with the literary tradition of the Greeks. In the Greek Testament he is the only real stylist of them all.

Something must be said about the Revelation of St. John the Divine, often called by its Greek name Apocalypse. In ordinary speech the word revelation generally implies some terrible revelation, and similarly Apocalypse, which was a popular kind of writing among the Greek-speaking Jews of the New Testament period, implied something terrible too. And in this Christian Apocalypse there is a great deal that is terrifying, and this is enhanced by the wildness of the language. There is an extraordinary disregard of the rules of grammar. The author may almost be said to make a rule for himself: When in doubt use the nominative. The whole effect cannot be reproduced in English. The truth is that, just as the Apocalypse relates what exceeds all probability and then offers no explanations, so the language disregards all rules and verges constantly on the incoherent. It is scarcely prose, but it is not poetry either.

There is thus a great variety of style in the Greek Testament. Yet the Koiné is a language which has lost many of the resources and refinements of the classical Greek, and that being so it is wonderful what Mark and Luke and John and Paul and the rest have made of it, and what the English versions have made of the Greek.

XV

THE GREEK TESTAMENT IN ENGLISH DRESS

and very handsomely apparelled

THE tradition of the Christian Church was and still is to have the Scriptures translated literally. Otherwise they will not be read with confidence, and in any case they need no heightening. Particularly in English they have a kind of majesty which Shakespeare and Milton have not equalled. Yet in many places they tend to be obscure, and in some places the language of the older Versions has grown obsolete. Scholars have not infrequently been tempted to try their hand at a new version which shall be more intelligible when it is read out or convey more of what the original means.

To see how far they have succeeded it will be useful to give a passage of the Greek in a number of different English versions. I choose for several good reasons a famous passage which occurs at II Cor. 4.17-5.1. It has the advantage of not being vexed by variant readings of the Greek text. It has one or two phrases where the idiom does not naturally lend itself

to translation into English. It contains a sentence or two
where once the right translation has been found it seems impossible that it could be bettered. And it expresses a noble
confession of faith in conformity with the best in pagan philosophy as well as in Christian theology. It is the most Platonic
of all Paul's utterances. Here it is in the English of

A.	William Tyndale	1526
B.	The Authorised Version	1611
C.	Daniel Mace	1729
D.	The Revised Version	1881
E.	Richard Francis Weymouth	1903
F.	James Moffatt	1913
G.	In Basic English	1941
H.	Ronald A. Knox	1945

1526 *Tyndale*. For our exceeding tribulation which is
momentary and light prepareth an exceeding and an eternal
weight of glory unto us while we look not on the things which
are seen but on the things which are not seen. For things
which are seen are temporal: and things which are not seen
are eternal. We know surely if our earthy mansion wherein
we now dwell were destroyed, we have a building ordained
of God, an habitation not made with hands, but eternal in
heaven.

1611 *A.V.* For our light affliction, which is but for a
moment, worketh for us a far more exceeding and eternal
weight of glory: while we look not at the things which are
seen, but at the things which are not seen: for the things which
are seen are temporal, but the things which are not seen are
eternal. For we know that if our earthly house of this tabernacle were dissolved, we have a building of God, an house not
made with hands, eternal in the heavens.

1729 *Mace*. For the light affliction, which I at present suffer,
will be infinitely overbalanced by an eternal weight of glory:
for I have no regard to the things which are visible, but to such
as are invisible: since visible things are temporary, but the
invisible are eternal. For I know, that if my body, which is
but a tent for my sojourning upon earth, were dissolved, I
have what is not fram'd by human art, but by the divine
architect, a mansion eternal in the heavens.

51

1881 *R.V.* For our light affliction which is for the moment worketh for us more and more exceedingly an eternal weight of glory: while we look not at the things which are seen, but at the things which are not seen: for the things which are seen are temporal: but the things which are not seen are eternal. For we know that if the earthly house of our tabernacle be dissolved, we have a building from God, a house not made with hands, eternal, in the heavens.

1903 *Weymouth.* For this our light and transitory burden of suffering is achieving for us a preponderating, yes, a vastly preponderating, and eternal weight of glory: while we look not at things seen, but things unseen; for things seen are temporary, but things unseen are eternal. For we know that if this poor tent, our earthly house, is taken down, we have in heaven a building which God has provided, a house not built by human hands, but eternal.

1913 *Moffatt.* The slight trouble of the passing hour results in a solid glory past all comparison, for those of us whose eyes are on the unseen, not on the seen: for the seen is transient, the unseen eternal. I know that if this earthly tent is taken down, I get a home from God, made by no human hands, eternal in the heavens.

1941 *Basic.* For our present trouble which is only for a short time, is working out for us a much greater weight of glory; while our minds are not on the things which are seen, but on the things which are not seen: for the things which are seen are for a time; but the things which are not seen are eternal. For we are conscious that if this our tent of flesh is taken down, we have a building from God, a house not made with hands, eternal, in heaven.

1945 *Knox.* (Translated from the Vulgate). This light and momentary affliction brings with it a reward multiplied every way, loading us with everlasting glory; if only we will fix our eyes on what is unseen, not on what we can see. What we can see lasts but for a moment; what is unseen is eternal. Once this earthly tent-dwelling of ours has come to an end, God, we are sure, has a solid building waiting for us, a dwelling not made with hands, that will last eternally in heaven.

These passages really tell their own story, yet a few obser-
vations may not be amiss. We see at once the difference between a translation and a paraphrase. The Greek towards the
end says quite simply, *a building from God, a house un-hand-
made.* A.V. hardly deviates from this in saying *a building of
God, a house not made with hands.* And we have only to look
at the later versions to see that, where they have altered this,
they have not improved it except that R.V. has got very slightly
nearer to the Greek by putting *from God* for *of God*.

This particular phrase, *a house not made with hands,* also
illustrates the rather important point that English loses nothing by being written in words of one syllable with their dignity
enhanced only occasionally by a long word. A.V. improves
on Tyndale by substituting *house* for *habitation,* but Tyndale's
not made with hands has not been and indeed could not be
bettered. A little further up Tyndale has 33 successive words
where only one has more than one syllable, and that is the
word *temporal* which came from the Vulgate, it is curious that
Knox does not retain it. Greek and Latin are not nearly so
much given to monosyllables. In the whole passage A.V. has
72 monosyllables and 14 other words. The Greek has 19
monosyllables and 36 other words. The Latin has 22 monosyllables and 40 other words. And the English would in fact
be rather better for more monosyllables. It would be closer
to the sense if instead of *our earthly house* we had *the house
which we have while we are on earth.*

The Basic English is confined to a vocabulary of 1,000 words
of which 850 are those which were selected by the promoters
as basic to the language, 50 are special Bible words, and 100
are listed as giving most help in the reading of English verse.
A translation within such limits is really only a curiosity,
though it might be useful in the mission field. But in this particular passage the result is not at all bad, and would be good if
it were worked over and a few non-basic words substituted
here and there and those not necessarily more elaborate ones.
We know would be a great improvement on *we are conscious.*
To attempt a Basic version sometimes compels the translator
to clear his mind, always a good thing in itself.

Finally there are two phrases in the Greek which are really
difficult to translate. The passage begins by saying *For the
momentary light element of affliction by the standard of excess
unto excess worketh an eternal weight of glory*. Tyndale takes
this to mean that excessively light affliction prepares an exces-

sive weight of glory. But A.V., correcting this on the view that the double use of *excess* was just a way of being emphatic, says *far more exceeding*. The other attempts here are all interesting. Mace says *infinitely overbalanced by an eternal weight*. R.V. says *more and more exceedingly*. Weymouth says *a preponderating, yea, a vastly preponderating and eternal weight*. Moffatt says *glory past all comparison*. Basic can't say it at all apparently. Knox says *a reward multiplied every way*. Of these attempts R.V. and Weymouth have the merit of repeating the same word twice as in the Greek, but *preponderating* will hardly do as an epithet of *weight*.

A greater difficulty still is where A.V. says *if our earthly house of this tabernacle were dissolved*. This does not mean much in itself, yet R.V. only ventured on a trifling alteration. Later versions have introduced the word *tent* which is what is intended by *tabernacle*, but the difficulty is that Greeks in Paul's time could speak of the tent of the body without further explanation. We speak of the bodily *frame*, but not easily of the bodily *tent*. *Integument* is a possibility, but the problem of translation is really insoluble. And in any case *dissolved* is not very suitable. The Greek word so translated is the one used over and over again of our Lord destroying the temple. If the word *tent* is used, *taken down* as in Weymouth, Moffatt, and Basic is suitable instead of *dissolved*. Yet *dissolved* may have been the right word in 1611, when A.V. put it in place of Tyndale's *destroyed*. For just about the very same time Shakespeare was writing

> The cloud-capped towers, the gorgeous palaces,
> The solemn temples, the great globe itself,
> Yea, all which it inherit, shall *dissolve,*
> And, like this insubstantial pageant faded,
> Leave not a rack behind. (*Tempest* IV, i.)

54

XVI

EPISTLES

in which are some things hard to be understood

THE word Epistle means a Letter, and is mainly applied to the collection of letters which compose about one-third of the New Testament. There are however many other collections of letters in the world besides. The word Gospel on the other hand is applied precisely to the first four books of the New Testament, and there are no other gospels in the world except two or three tawdry imitations of these four. The Gospels are unparalleled.

It is safe to say that wherever there is writing there will soon be letters, and it is characteristic of letters that the style is somewhat informal. Many people have written letters with an eye to publication, but they have always tried to give them a spontaneous and informal air. The great collections of antiquity are those of Plato, Cicero and Pliny. But the Plato letters were written some centuries before the New Testament, and the others are in Latin. To find out what letters of St. Paul's time were usually like we must look among the papyri, where we shall find heaps of them. They are quite like the letters of our own time. A boy who has lately joined the army writes home to say that he is all right and his mother need not trouble to send him anything. A man writes to borrow money, or to try and recover some he has lent. Women write about servants. And so forth.

But a good letter has so much charm and ease that people who have something to say to the public have often been tempted to express their thoughts in letter form, and if they are long letters they often print them like pamphlets instead of sending them through the post. The Epistles of the New Testament all have something of this artificial character with the exception of Philemon, II and III John. These three are personal and occasional letters. So are I and II Timothy and Titus in a sense. They are addressed to individuals, but with their congregations in view. They are personal letters, but they are meant to be read out. The principal Epistles (Rom.,

I and II Cor., Eph., I Pet., Jas., Heb.) are addressed to large communities of Christians. The writers speak in the first person to their readers in the second person, e.g. *I would not have you ignorant* (I Cor. 12.1). They normally have a beginning and an ending of a personal kind. They have plenty of personal feeling in them, they are far from being detached. They are often written straight off the reel, or more probably dictated, for the ancients quite commonly employed stenographers. In Rom. 16.22 the scribe Tertius writes a sentence or two as from himself, *I Tertius who wrote (down) this epistle salute you in the Lord,* perhaps because he was personally known to the Roman readers and Paul was not. Paul must have been writing or dictating *extempore* in I Cor. 1.14-16: *I thank God that I baptised none of you but Crispus and Gaius, lest any should say that I had baptised in my own name. And I baptised also the house of Stephanas: besides, I know not whether I baptised any other.*

Ancient letter writers almost always begin with wishing 'health' to their correspondents. Paul invariably wishes them 'grace and peace', to which in I and II Tim. and Titus he adds 'mercy'. He names the people he is writing to as *the saints* in such a place, though in Ephesians the two best manuscripts (ℵ B) and Origen omit '*in Ephesus*' so perhaps it was a circular letter. It has no personal conclusion. Hebrews on the other hand has lost its opening words of greeting if it ever had any, but it has a perfunctory conclusion as of a letter, though it is in truth an essay. Most ancient letters end with a brief Farewell. Paul sends greetings to individuals and concludes with what we should call a Grace, of which the most celebrated is *The grace of our Lord Jesus Christ, and the love of God, and the fellowship of the Holy Ghost be with you all* (II Cor. 13.14). To Romans he appends a very long list of greetings to individuals, although he had never been in Rome at the time.

Having got over the preliminaries Paul breaks out in a huge sentence which would not be tolerated in a literary work. These huge sentences go much better in Greek than in the English Authorised Version. We must come to a full stop before long in English, but Greek with its more various declensions and conjugations, its larger array of pronouns, and its greater fluidity can carry on for a long time. In a passage of about 30 lines between the 9th verse and the 24th verse of Colossians 1 no full stop is called for in the Greek. The printed texts all insert full stops, but there is no one place where the Received Text, the Revisers' Text, and Westcott and Hort agree in putting one, because there is no one place where a full stop is wholly appropriate.

After a somewhat confused and breathless beginning Paul seems to see what it is he really wants to say. He selects one or two of the many ideas he was so full of at the start, and expounds them sometimes logically and sometimes indignantly, sometimes faultily and sometimes persuasively. This is Jewish passion in a Greek dress. And finally he seems to calm down and give very practical advice on the Christian life and character. It is probably true to say that he has had more influence on Christian conduct than on Christian theology. He has certainly provided a great many of the terms in which both are discussed. When he speaks of women, he is nearly always hopelessly wide of the mark, but so were nearly all Greek writers except Sophocles.

The non-Pauline epistles give the impression of being modelled on Paul, except perhaps James which is very dour, and I John which defies analysis and with II and III John has all the appearance of being a collection of literary fragments. But the fragments all have the unmistakable style of John. It is perhaps fair to say that in the Greek they are less remote than in the English, but somehow they seem less impressive too, Greek being in some ways a more matter-of-fact language than English.

XVII

GOSPELS

a new kind of book

IF the Epistles are rather unusual specimens of an ordinary kind of writing, the Gospels on the other hand are a kind of writing all to themselves. For more than a century now the scholars have been trying the experiment of approaching them as ordinary books and seeing what can be made of them that way. But at last it is being realised that treated like that the Gospels will not yield the answer to any of the real questions which they raise. All that can be said is that the recollections men have of a great teacher usually consist largely of anecdotes many of which are only vaguely attached to a particular time or place, and this is in the main true of the great Teacher Jesus of Nazareth. To that extent they are ordinary. But the anecdotes are for the most part so extraordinary that they would scarcely be thought worth lingering over if it were not that they also seem so natural and are combined with the most startling and attractive teaching about the character of God and the nature of man.

The form in which the record of Jesus is presented has several remarkable features about it. The Gospels are not biographies, and they are not story-books, and they are not exactly history. Fundamentally they are text books and teaching manuals. As long as there were many alive who had known Jesus in the flesh, the teaching about his life and person were given orally by those who were *eye-witnesses and ministers of the word* (Luke 1.2). But as the generation of the Apostles passed away, there was need to record in writing what the Christians thought should be remembered and handed on *of all that Jesus began both to do and teach* (Acts 1.1). The Gospels are the outcome of this need, and they all have the same general outline. They are in fact *the* Gospel according to four different people. All four Evangelists fit the acts and sayings of Jesus into the framework of a ministry of preaching in the course of which he travelled about in Galilee and from time to time made his way to Jerusalem. They represent him as being accompanied by disciples and followed about by crowds. They all make out this Ministry as having been so provocative that it led to the Crucifixion. The last days before the Crucifixion and that event itself are described in very considerable detail and with some minute circumstances in the latter part of the narrative; this part is called the Passion. All the Gospels conclude with some account of the Resurrection. All agree that Jesus worked miracles of healing and brought dead men to life again. All agree that he taught by parables. All agree that a few days before his death he delivered a long address on the end of the age and a day of judgment. They all give the substance of this address at some length (Matt. 24: Mark 13: Luke 21: John 15-16). But they do not all agree as to what he said. The first three Gospels exhibit a general agreement against the fourth Gospel at this point and at many others.

58

This creates two problems. The first concerns the relation of the first three Gospels to one another. That three separate books should be so much alike and yet in many ways so different makes one ask whether any one of them is to be regarded as more authoritative than the others. In order to answer this question the three Gospels have been compared and examined very closely indeed, and to do this it was necessary to arrange the texts side by side. Such an arrangement is called a SYNOPSIS; not because it is a summary, but because synopsis really means 'a seeing all together', as the Greek lexicon tells us. The three Evangelists are for the same reason called the Synoptists, and the problem they create is called the Synoptic problem. A good synopsis in English has been made by J. M. Thompson and published by the Clarendon Press at Oxford under the title *The Synoptic Gospels*. But of course an examination of the Greek is absolutely necessary if any certainty is to be had, because conclusions can only be reached by the cumulative effect of many small details all pointing in the same direction, and these details often depend on the Greek.

One such small point may be cited in illustration of this. At Matt. 7.23 and Luke 13.27 we have a quotation from Ps. 6.8 *Away from me, all ye that work vanity.* The R.V. gives in Matt. *Depart from me, ye that work iniquity,* and in Luke *Depart from me, all ye workers of iniquity.* The difference between *that work iniquity* and *all ye workers of iniquity* indicates fairly enough the difference in the corresponding Greek. What the English does not show is that Matthew and Luke do not use the same Greek word for *depart.* Luke uses the same word as the Septuagint, thus suggesting that he is accustomed to the Old Testament in Greek; Matthew perhaps translates from the Hebrew. From this single instance you could prove nothing, but if there were a number of other similar instances, you would infer that Matthew is a Jew and Luke a Gentile, which may be important for the general interpretation of their works.

The best synopsis of the Greek text is that of Albert Huck published at Tübingen, and also in England for those who know no German (B. H. Blackwell, Oxford).

It is now generally agreed that Mark's Gospel is the earliest and that Matthew and Luke both made use of it in compiling theirs. In addition each had some source peculiar to himself, and they also had a common source perhaps some 200 verses in extent which Mark did not use. This source is called Q, and consists almost entirely of sayings of Jesus, though it also contains one miracle (Matt. 8.5: Luke 7.2). It would be the earliest authority for the teaching of Jesus, if we had it, but no trace of an actual document at all like it has so far been discovered. A very great respect must therefore be accorded to Mark, though, alongside their common deference to him, each of the other synoptists has his own particular contribution to make. Mark is the least consciously adorned by any literary style, yet his vivid interest in what he portrays makes the earliest Gospel a most admirable piece of writing. Tradition says that his information is based on what St. Peter told him. Matthew arranges his material very carefully with a view to its being learnt and remembered. And in fact, when people tell a Gospel story in ordinary life, they usually tell it in a form which is nearer to Matthew's version than to the others. We say the Lord's Prayer as he gives it. Some of the matter which is peculiar to Matthew has the character of Jewish folklore. The vision of judgment which is commonly called ' The Sheep and the Goats' is most majestic (Matt. 25.31-46). Luke is more literary, though not more like secular literature. He loves a moving story, and is a very good judge of one. He alone records the parables of the Prodigal Son (Luke 15) and the Good Samaritan (Luke 10) and the story of the Penitent Thief (Luke 23) and of the Disciples going to Emmaus (Luke 24). But some will feel (as I do) that this Gospel is just slightly 'touched up'.

It has been estimated that about four-fifths of Matthew's 1,068 verses and two-thirds of Luke's 1,149 verses are derived from Mark, and where they are on common ground they often agree word for word. But it is not certain that they actually copied Mark out. The stories may have assumed already a traditional form in which they were told by word of mouth; and this form tended to fall into one of several patterns. It has been the object of what is called FORM CRITICISM to identify and classify these patterns into which they fell before they were written down. But what of it? You must tell a story some way or another.

The relation of the Synoptics to the Gospel of St. John presents another problem. John is the great enigma of the New Testament, and a vast amount has been written on this Johannine problem. It is easy to exaggerate the differences between him and the other three. But he has certainly remembered or discovered a different strain in the teachings of Jesus, and his own meditations have given his Gospel a unified and individual style. He uses less than 1,000 distinct Greek words altogether, but beneath the apparent simplicity there are profound notions about the life of God which the other Gospels hardly catch at all. Nevertheless there are a few verses in the Synoptics which have unmistakably a Johannine sound (Matt. 11.27 *All things are delivered unto me of my Father, and no man knoweth the Son but the Father; neither knoweth any man the Father save the Son, and he to whomsoever the Son will reveal him.* Mark 9.37: Luke 9.48; 10.22). It may be perhaps that the kind of teaching we find in John was given to all the Apostles, but only remembered by this particular one of them except to a very small extent. It is difficult to resist the impression that John is often further away from history than the others, but possibly nearer to the heart of the matter; and when he comes to the Passion narrative he is probably the most historical of the four. He has produced a masterpiece in Greek, though he does not strike one as being a great master of the Greek language. His relation to the other Evangelists was thus described by Clement of Alexandria at the end of the second century:

'Finally John, being conscious that the material aspect of things had been made plain in the (other) Gospels, at the urgent request of the disciples and under the inspiration of the Spirit, composed a spiritual Gospel.'

(Eusebius. H.E.VI. xiv.7, quoting from the lost *Hypotyposes* of Clement).

The word Gospel is interesting. It is the old English for 'good news' (god spel), and this is just what the Greek original means also. It is used, like the Greek, for two different things, first for the general teaching of Jesus Christ, the message of salvation as it is called; and secondly, as an almost technical name for the first four books of the New Testament. The words that go with it however are not of Anglo-Saxon origin, but come from the Greek either directly or through the Vulgate. We call the writer of a gospel an Evangelist, and we call preaching the gospel evangelising. In German the Gospel is *Evangelium* and in French it is *l'Evangile*. So Gospel is a peculiarly English word. It has often been used as though it stood for Goddes Spel, God's word, but this was not so at the first. (See N.E.D. under Gospel.) The word Gospeller was in

61

old times used for Evangelist, but is now almost confined to one who reads the Gospel in church, though the particular phrase 'hot gospeller' has survived for a hot-headed preacher of the Gospel.

The Greek word is interesting too. It occurs in Homer, meaning a 'reward for bringing good news' and subsequently in classical Greek authors in the same sense. But by New Testament times it had come to mean the good news itself and is so used by Plutarch and Lucian. Paul uses it very frequently in that sense and probably introduced it into the Christian community. Its use specifically for one of the four Gospels may be due to Mark in whose Gospel it is the third word: (*The*) *beginning of-the Gospel of Jesus Christ, the son of God* (Mark 1.1).

XVIII

THE ROMAN EMPIRE

in the first century

WHEN you are reading a book about a foreign country, it helps very much towards the understanding of it to know the country or its language. It makes what happens seem much more natural. When I am reading Dostoevsky's novels, for example, I always wish I knew Russian, for in Russian I expect they would not seem half so mad as they do in English. Similarly a knowledge of Greek will contribute to making the New Testament, or rather the movement it sprang from, more real and natural, and to know something of the country is useful in the same way.

If it were only a question of the Gospels, we should want to know about Palestine, and a Baedeker or some other modern guide-book to Palestine is in fact one of the best aids to the study of the Bible. But the New Testament as a whole is not about Palestine only or even mostly. It is about the Roman Empire. You might say that the New Testament contains two parts: first, the history of the spread of Christ's preaching from Palestine to Rome and through the intervening countries, and in the second part, the literature that was occasioned in the process. The whole story lies within the Roman Empire, and all the literature was written in the Empire, and in so far as it consisted of letters was addressed to people within the Empire. A good slice of the story belongs to Rome, and more still to Judaea, and to various portions of the great high road, the *via Egnatia*, which runs from one to the other. A section of it (Acts 27-28) gives a vivid picture of a voyage which went the whole length of the Eastern Mediterranean from Sidon to Brindisi. To read of this in the language which you would have heard on every side throughout this whole area is to get near to the feeling of the events and places. And to know something of the Roman Empire as well is to get nearer still.

And the Roman Empire was nothing less than all the lands that border on the Mediterranean brought under one system of government with the Roman emperor at its head. Its writ ran far inland too and across the narrow seas to the Firth of Forth and at the other extremity to the river Euphrates. And this Empire was no remote idea, lifted high above the realities of life, as it was in the early Middle Ages. It confronted everyone. Its laws were there to be obeyed, its officials were there to ensure obedience. Its taxes and tributes were paid. Its power was exhibited by legions stationed in almost every province, twenty-five to thirty of them in all. Local magistracies and historic assemblies were preserved and had their duties prescribed to them, but they had to mind their own business. When the Emperors were not lunatic, which Caligula, Claudius, and Nero all were each in his own peculiar way (A.D. 37-68), they kept in touch with everything and provided a kind of rough justice which was highly valued. They managed to have some kind of order kept even in Palestine. All this was based in the last resort on military power. The title of Emperor means 'the commander-in-chief'. But alongside this military power there was an elaborate civil service which had been organised by the level-headed genius of Augustus who was in supreme control from 31 B.C. to A.D. 14.

It is impossible here to survey the whole Empire. Let us consider two different parts of it and see what the Greek Testament tells about them. Judaea shall be one part and Macedonia the other.

For purposes of administration the Empire was divided into provinces, just as India is or was. The peaceful provinces were governed by pro-consuls whom we may picture as something like ex-cabinet ministers. These provinces, of which Sicily was one, were called senatorial provinces. But the provinces which required a military occupation were governed by pro-praetors, whom we may think of as successful generals. These were called imperial provinces. The governor of every province was in any case a senator. Now Palestine formed part of the province of Syria, and the seat of the pro-praetor's government was at Antioch. But one finds without surprise that Palestine was regarded as a portion of the province which required very special treatment. Some parts of it including Galilee were governed by kings and tetrarchs of the name and family of Herod, sort of Maharajahs and Rajahs, treated as equals by the Roman governors (Acts 25.13). Among these Herod the Great (37-4 B.C.) was very eminent, but soon after his death Judaea was under a series of Procurators or Agents of whom few were successful. For a good reason Pontius Pilate (A.D. 26-36) is the best known of them.

For the Emperor, the pro-praetor, and the procurator the Greek Testament has one common word and it means a Leader, a Duce, a Fuehrer. In Luke 3.1 an attempt is made to date the preaching of St. John Baptist by saying it was in the *Leadership* (the actual word is the *Hegemony*) of Tiberius Caesar, that is to say he was the emperor, but it also says that Pontius Pilate was *leading* in Judaea, that is to say he was pro-curator, though the interesting manuscript D thinks this is too good a word and says that he was 'acting as agent'. In Luke 2.2 it says that when Jesus was born Quirinius was *leading* in Syria, that is to say he was pro-praetor.

In Judaea there were a certain number of self-governing cities of which Jerusalem is one. The Gospel makes it clear that the Sanhedrin, as the native council was called, had much power there and was much feared. Yet its power was strictly limited, and it went in constant fear of being suppressed (John 11.48: compare Acts 19.40). The narrative of the Crucifixion turns on the fact that the Sanhedrin could not condemn anyone to death.

The administration of the province of Syria being thus decentralised, the headquarters of the Government of Palestine were at Caesarea, and the palace of the Herods there was used as an official residence and called the Praetorium or Government House (Acts 23.35). There were three legions in Syria and three in Palestine round about the year A.D. 50, 30,000 men in all perhaps. These were fully armed infantry. The country itself provided the auxiliaries, such as those two hundred 'spearmen' in Acts 23.23—if spearmen they be, for Luke gives them an odd name which was probably local or regimental, and suggests something like 'Right-handers'. The English version is as a matter of fact not very successful at translating political and military terms precisely, but this is partly because even in the Greek these terms are only attempts at Greek equivalents for the Latin. In some cases they are only transliterations. Centurion (Mark 15.39) and legion (Mark 5.9: Luke 8.30: Matt. 26.53) and colony (Acts 16.12) appear in Greek and English alike, and belong to neither language. They are all three of them Latin words.

That there was an army of occupation in Palestine is shown in the plainest way in Luke 3. Amongst various classes of people who came to John Baptist to ask what they should do, the soldiers asked *And what shall we do?* John answered (Luke 3.14): *Do violence to no man, neither accuse any falsely: and be content with your wages.* Now it is ridiculous to tell a soldier to do violence to no man. That is the very thing he is paid to do. But what John said is eminently appropriate to policemen. They must not use unnecessary force, they must not bring false accusations, and they must not go on strike.

It is time to turn to Macedonia. This was a full-blown province dating back to 168 B.C. When Christianity reached it about A.D. 50 it comprised most of what we call Albania, the southern extremities of Jugo-Slavia and Bulgaria, and the north-eastern part of Greece. In A.D. 44, after thirty years as an imperial province, it had once again become a senatorial province. This means that the military situation was no longer one of urgency. From east to west through the province ran the Egnatian road to Rome, and on this road lay Philippi and Thessalonica, the chief places visited by St. Paul. Thessalonica was the capital. Philippi had been the chief town of one of the four districts into which the province was originally divided (Acts 16.12).

Philippi was the first place in Europe in which Paul preached. It is called a *colony*, that is to say it had been set apart for the settlement of old soldiers, primarily those who had fought in the battle of Philippi in 42 B.C. A colony implied a considerable measure of self-government. Here St. Paul's preaching brought him, as it usually did, into conflict with the authorities. The case was referred to some magis-

65   MGT—C

trates who were probably not of the highest rank, though they bore the high-sounding title of 'the generals'. These magistrates lost their heads, at any rate they rent their garments (Acts 16.22), and ordered Paul and Silas to be beaten and put in prison. Here an earthquake occurred which presently led the generals to send their marshals ('rod-holders' it says) to release them (16.35). But at this point the imperial government comes in. *They have beaten us openly uncondemned, being Romans,* says St. Paul, *and have cast us into prison: and now do they thrust us out privily? nay verily; but let them come themselves and fetch us out.* And the 'generals' came and fetched them out with entreaties. It was no small thing to be a Roman citizen, as Paul was. And of this the full proof comes later, when Paul asserts the right of every Roman citizen with his appeal unto Caesar. *Thou hast appealed unto Caesar,* comes the answer presently from Festus the procurator of Judaea, *unto Caesar thou shalt go* (Acts 25.12). And go he did.

One of the difficulties with which the first Christian missionaries had to contend was that they so often appeared to be proclaiming a new King, and, although the equivalent of King in Greek (as in Latin) did not denote the highest rank and was not a title of the Emperor, it was regarded with the greatest dislike by the Roman government. And this was heightened in the case of Jesus by the fact that he was called *Lord* and *Son of God,* and these were amongst the divine honours claimed for the reigning Caesar and for him alone. The fear of Caesar and the Romans is everywhere in the New Testament. The Pharisees in Jerusalem think that, if Jesus prevails, the Romans will come and take away their place and nation (John 11.48). The Jews try to persuade Pontius Pilate with the plea, *If thou let this man go, thou art not Caesar's friend,* and they soon succeed (John 19.12). In Thessalonica the accusation against the Christians is that they *all do contrary to the decrees of Caesar, saying that there is another King, one Jesus* (Acts 17.7). The town-clerk of Ephesus tells the crowd that they *are in danger to be called into account for this day's uproar* (Acts 19.40). He has the Romans in mind, and the thought sobers the crowd at once, and they disperse.

On the other hand the imperial government was greatly respected as well as feared. There is no doubt that the imperial provinces were, generally speaking, better governed than

66

the senatorial provinces, and the provincials much preferred imperial rule. At Caesarea the procurator sits on his dais or judgment-seat and Paul being brought before him describes himself as standing at Caesar's judgment seat where he ought to be judged (Acts 25.10). The officials, though sometimes cruel (Luke 13.1), seem to be painstaking and to aim at being just. Gallio, who on a celebrated occasion 'couldn't care less' was governor of a senatorial province, and is rightly called pro-consul and not pro-praetor in Acts 18.12. The title *deputy of Achaia* in A.V. gives no idea of his importance. He was the governor-general. At another level the eight centurions of the Roman army who appear in the New Testament are all men who do their duty conscientiously and considerately. They had all risen from the ranks; there were very few officers in the Roman army who had not.

Paul in the later chapter of Acts has one great wish. It is to see Rome (Acts 19.21). He only gets there as a prisoner, but while in custody he is liberally treated, and writing to the Philippians he sends this message of greeting: *All the Christians here send their greetings, especially those in Caesar's house* (Phil. 4.22). He must have the Roman government in view when he writes in Rom. 13.1-7 these striking comments on our Lord's advice to render unto Caesar the things that are Caesar's. *There is no power but of God; the powers that be are ordained of God. Whosoever therefore resisteth the power resisteth the ordinance of God. . . . He beareth not the sword in vain. For he is the minister of God. . . . Wherefore ye must needs be subject, not only for wrath, but also for conscience sake. . . . Render therefore to all their dues: tribute to whom tribute is due; custom to whom custom; fear to whom fear; honour to whom honour.* You can hardly say more of the government than that.

The Roman Empire was one of the great facts to be reckoned with in the earliest days of Christianity. It was not long before Christian thinkers saw in it the mark of a providential design, and looking back we cannot say that they were wrong. For it gave free access to a world which was looking for new gods, and Roman rule and Greek speech were the two great instruments which that world itself put into the hands of the Church.

Part III

PHILOLOGUS: OR THE WORDS

PHILOLOGUS: OR THE WORDS

a dialogue reported

In the Precincts of Westminster Abbey there is a garden—
a large garden, and along one side of it there are three houses
in which there used to live three Canons, of whom one was
a good scholar, and one was a good preacher, but the third,
Canon Lomax by name, had not attained to be either a good
scholar or a good preacher. Perhaps he was a humorist, for
it was said that he had composed his own epitaph and had set
down of himself in it that *He read much poetry and studied
in the Greek Testament a little.* And if he set down that he
set down what was true.

Now it happened not so long ago that I was sitting in the
garden with this Canon Lomax one afternoon in the month
of July, and we were admiring a couple of those tall plane
trees which do so well in London. And that led him to
observe that we were like Socrates and Phaedrus in Plato's
Dialogue who sat under a very tall and spreading plane tree to
discourse of rhetoric. And that made me tell him how I had
been present at a long discussion in the garden only the day
before, arising out of some popular lectures he had given in
the Abbey on the Greek Testament.

What did they say, my dear man? he asked.

Well, I said, it began with someone asserting that it was not
much use knowing Greek for the purpose of reading the Greek
Testament, because it did not tell you much that was not in
the English. But someone else hotly denied this, and said it
made all the difference in the world. So we all fell to discussing what difference.

And how much difference was there in the end?

Well, I should say we Grecians thought we came to know
the exact meaning of a good many words through the Greek,
and had some sort of an outline of New Testament teaching, which we could not have got nearly so well from the
English.

That was certainly something, Canon Lomax said. Tell me
some more.

Now this rather embarrassed me, because as a matter of fact I had made some notes of the words we discussed, and, as it was only the day before, I could remember a good deal of what was said. But I did not know if he really wanted to hear a lot of it. So I said that it would take a good long time to tell it all.

Excellent, he said. We have all the afternoon before us, and Prudence will give us some tea presently. Let us go into the house.

So we went into the house, and sat in what he calls the Saloon, and I told what I remembered of the talk. But as some things were said which did not wholly tally with the Canon's lectures, I disguised my companions at the discussion by the names of some of the very early Christians.

I had better introduce you to the company at once, I said to him. Salute Asyncritus, Phlegon, Hermas, Patrobas, Hermes. Salute Philologus and Julia and Nereus.

What a lot, he said, and a woman amongst them!

Yes, I answered, your daughter Prudence, in fact. But I shall call her Julia. She did not say much, but she might confirm or correct my report of the proceedings.

And which of them is you? he asked me.

None of them, I answered, because I hardly said a word. I was busy taking my notes. But all the rest had a share in it, some more and some less. Philologus certainly took the lead, while Hermas and Hermes, who are twins and not seventeen years of age, mostly ran messages and did odd jobs, as you will see.

It was really old Nereus who began the discussion, I continued. He said it was quite interesting to hear about old books being written by hand and how they were copied and circulated, and what they looked like and what sort of mistakes they had in them and all that, but after all it didn't make any difference to him. The good old English Bible was good enough for him.

But to this Philologus answered that there was no question of good enough. Only the best you could get would do. And the Greek Testament was at any rate older than the English Bible, and better too, because it must have lost a good deal more than it had gained by being translated, even if you allow that it gains something in its splendid English dress. And therefore, he said, he was all for the good old Greek Testament because it was both older and better.

Well, I grant you it is older, said Phlegon, breaking in, but what exactly do you mean by saying that it is better?

I mean, Philologus answered, that it is nearer what the Apostles wrote, in fact you may quite reasonably say that it is what the Apostles wrote.

Oh, bother the Apostles, said Asyncritus. They lived a long time ago. It's only by reading the Bible that you can know about Christianity, and I shall never know enough to read it properly in Greek. I really don't know any.

But even a little Greek will take you somewhere, said Philologus. What a present-day parson teaches, if he knows his job, is surprisingly the same as what the Apostles taught, and all the special words he uses except one are either from the Latin or the Greek, and nearly all the Latin ones came into use because they translated a word in the Greek Testament.

Will you illustrate that, said Phlegon, for I don't really know just what you have in mind.

Well, supposing somebody comes across the expression Works of Supererogation, said Philologus. He is quite likely to go and ask his parson what supererogation is. And the parson might tell him it means something like an extra effort. And if he asked why, he might tell him that it is derived from a word that comes out of the Latin Bible at the place in the parable of the Good Samaritan where it says *Whatsoever thou spendest more*. And the Greek original of the same passage tells you here that this long Latin legal term Supererogation is represented by quite an ordinary Greek word, and ought to mean quite simply 'spending more'. Of course, it comes to mean a great deal else, but that's the starting-point. That's one instance. Take the word Cosmos for a more important one.

Wait a minute, said Phlegon. What is the one special word the parson uses that isn't either Greek or Latin?

Atonement, said Philologus, which is making people *at one*, and from the expression 'making atonement' you work back to 'atoning for something' which is a good long way from the original idea—all English haziness and laziness of thought, I call it.

Is the Greek language less hazy then? Phlegon asked.

Yes, a great deal. It has a great many words but very few of them have been imported from other languages, so you don't get so many pairs of words meaning almost the same thing, so many synonyms I mean, as you do in English.

73

But do you?

Yes, 'acknowledge and confess', 'dissemble and cloke', 'labour and work', for example.

Yes, so you do.

In Greek on the other hand you can make compounds much more easily and get variety of meaning that way, though I won't say there are no synonyms in Greek. There are two words for 'new' for instance, and it is hard to give them different meanings, but it is always worth while trying to distinguish the sense of two words in Greek, when it would often be fanciful to do it in English. But I wasn't talking about pairs of words. I was asking about Cosmos.

Well, said Patrobas, the father of the twins, who is a very learned but rather precise person, what you said was, Take Cosmos.

Take Cosmos and double it, said Asyncritus rather pettishly, and then add six to it.

And the result is what you first thought of, said Phlegon, because the Cosmos is infinite.

Asyncritus made nothing of that, but Philologus said to Phlegon, Then you at any rate know some Greek, since it seems that you know that the Cosmos is infinite.

Naturally I know the Cosmos is the Universe, because that is what people often call it.

Oh, so you know the Latin too, the Universum or Sumtotal. And of course you know the English as well?

I suppose it is the World, he said.

Yes, you are right. We use all three words, the World, the Universe, and the Cosmos, and all with a slightly different meaning in the back of our minds. For 'World' in English originally meant 'man's life', and then it came to mean what he is aware of, the world about us, as we say. And the word Universe seems to emphasise the oneness of this world. And the Cosmos—what does the Greek word Cosmos mean?

It means the World, said Phlegon.

But Philologus said it would be truer to say that it stands for the World. If you had learnt Greek, he said to Phlegon, you would know that it really means Order, and then comes to mean—among other things—the World, because the World is constituted in such a wonderful order. And it means Beauty too, because the Greek thought Order was a special kind of Beauty, as indeed it is.

74

Well, that was a very cunning thought of the Greeks, Phlegon said. How did they come by it, and when?

The history of it is rather curious, replied Philologus. In early times, it might be in the ninth century before Christ, some tribes from the north-west of Greece began to move eastward. Some of these reached Attica and Athens. Then contingents of them crossed the Aegean sea and established themselves in the west of Asia Minor. They were called Ionians, and about the beginning of the seventh century they took to indulging in speculations about the world. They laid the foundations of Greek science, and their ideas were transported back again to Greece and southern Italy, which was then full of Greek cities, and there they found their mature development. These old Greeks, being very imaginative and very inquisitive, soon asked themselves the three questions which the existence of the world naturally puts into men's heads when they come to think about it.

What questions, please? Phlegon asked.

The first is, How does it work? from which it is difficult to separate the second, Where did it come from? And the third question is, What is it for? The Greeks from the beginning of the sixth century B.C. were very much interested in what the stuff might be of which the world is composed. The view largely prevailed that it was composed of what we still call the Four Elements, Earth, Air, Fire and Water, but some thought it all came originally from one Element, though they did not agree as to which one it was. And they even got a stage further, and seemed to see that it was not any stuff at all that must account for it, but a unifying power or principle, since it all held together and was certainly all one World. Pythagoras was the first to call it an Order, a Cosmos, and this was about the end of the sixth century.

And I suppose Cosmos eventually became the accepted word for the World, said Phlegon, and got into the Greek Testament, just because it was the accepted word, and because the early Christians commonly spoke Greek.

Yes, they did all speak Greek, as their second language, if not as their first. The Roman Empire was bilingual, and in parts trilingual, as the inscription on the cross suggests, and Greek served as a *lingua franca*, the international language as you might say. But actually the Christians got their idea of the Cosmos from the Jewish religion and not from Greek philosophers and scientists. Up to a point the Greeks and the Jews came to the same conclusion. The Greeks came to think the world was one, and therefore there could ultimately be only one supreme God in charge of it, while the Jews came to think there was only one God and therefore there could only be one world. They got on to common ground from opposite directions. And the earliest Christians, being Jews, got to it the Jewish way. But you can't help noticing that when the world is spoken of in the New Testament, it is not its order or its beauty, but its wickedness that usually seems to be in mind. Christianity most decidedly disapproves of what it calls the world.

Yes, that's true, said Phlegon. It certainly is spoken of with great dislike and stands condemned.

Yes, nearly always, said Philologus. As for example *The wisdom of this world is foolishness with God,* or *The friendship of the world is enmity with God,* and so forth. And this opposition is most noticeable in St. John's writings. I should think he uses the word Cosmos as often as all the other Greek Testament writers put together. Hermas and Hermes, he said, go to the library and count up in the Concordance, and tell us the exact figures.

The twins ran off. And Patrobas said that he remembered a comment of Bishop Westcott which he thought he could quote, and it seemed to the point—the fundamental idea of Cosmos in St. John is that of the sum of created being which belongs to the sphere of human life as an ordered whole, considered apart from God. And Westcott adds a little further down: It is easy to see how the thought of an ordered whole relative to man and considered apart from God passes into that of the ordered whole *separated* from God. And it is easy to see from Westcott, Patrobas continued, that this separation soon leads on to the idea of the world setting itself up as the rival and enemy of God.

Yes, that is the point, agreed Philologus. I am so glad you seem to be so familiar with Westcott.

Yes, said Patrobas, of all modern English commentaries I ever saw, I think Westcott's *St. John* the most like the old Fathers. He did not know much about the language of the Greek Testament, he thought it was like classical Greek, only rather bad. But he often interpreted the thought profoundly.

Well, he has done it here anyway, Philologus answered. And of course it is St. John's attitude which has done most to settle the Christian attitude to the world, though the point of view of the other Gospels is really just the same if you examine it.

At this point Hermas and Hermes came back panting. How many times? Philologus asked.

Cosmos comes 182 times in the Greek Testament, said Hermas.

But I made it 184, said Hermes, and 101 of these times in St. John's writings, excluding the Revelation.

And how many times in the Revelation?

Three times only.

We'll leave that on one side, said Philologus. In any case it must be a favourite word with St. John. And there is no doubt that in his Gospel he represents the enmity between the World and God as shown in the clearest possible way by the Crucifixion of Jesus by the Jews. *He was in the world, and the world was made through him, and the world knew him not. He came unto his own, and his own received him not.* The whole Gospel of John is a set of variations on this theme.

Here Asyncritus interrupted to ask why Philologus said *The world was made through him,* when in the Bible it says *The world was made by him.* And Philologus said it was because he knew by the Greek that John did not mean that the Son made the world, but that the Creator made the world by means of the Son, or because of the Son, or with reference to the Son, and that *through him* would mean something like that, whereas *by him* would now mean something else, whatever it meant to the translators in 1611. But, Philologus went on, although the rejection of Christ by the world is John's constant theme, yet there are undertones. There were those who received him. And *As many as received him, to them gave he power to become the sons of God,* and again, *God so loved the world that he gave his only-begotten Son, that whosoever believeth on him should not perish, but have everlasting life.* This is good news for the world, a Gospel for the Cosmos. But it can hardly be understood unless you have the Jewish idea of creation in mind.

That is to say, Phlegon remarked, unless you have some answer to your second question about the world. Where did it come from?

Philologus assented. Precisely, he said, though the Jewish answer to the question, while it satisfied the Jews, I suppose, would not have satisfied most of the Greeks. You find it in the very beginning of the Old Testament, and it gives a picture

—almost a diagram—of creation without attempting to explain it. That would not have done for the Greeks, and it does not do for a great many minds to-day. But it did all right for the Apostles. They were content to believe that God (and there is only one God in view) created the world by his word and his will, and that he did it for his own pleasure, and *saw that it was very good*. And after all no one has got much further than that.

Except that the world isn't very good as a matter of fact, said Phlegon.

No, perhaps not, but a Greek would have said that even if there were signs of disorder in it, yet it still remains, generally speaking, a wonderful order, and a Jew would have said likewise that, though there was wickedness in it, it was obviously meant to be very good. And he had a picture of Eve and the Serpent and the Apple to fall back on to explain the existence of evil, though it was certainly not a very easy picture to make out. But it was just as easy as to say that Evil is a kind of good if we could only see it, or that it is a stage in the evolution of man. There is truth in all these ways of looking at it, though it still remains unexplained, and so does all existence in the end.

But anyway, said Patrobas, the Fall of Man, and our not being what we were meant to be, however you picture it, accounts for a lot.

Yes indeed, it does, Philologus agreed. And at any rate we still have to accept the Cosmos as a starting-point, whatever its history may have been. The Greek Testament speaks of *the foundation of the world* and *the beginning of the creation,* meaning much the same thing by both expressions. And St. Paul has put the argument for inferring the existence of a Creator God from the character of the Creation in a very striking sentence: *The invisible things of him from the creation of the world are clearly seen, being understood through the things that are made.* By *the things that are made* Paul means the Cosmos, and since the creation of the Cosmos it has been possible from it and in it, he says, to see *the invisible things of God,* and he goes on to define these invisible things as *his eternal power and Godhead.*

Philologus paused for a moment, and everyone looked thoughtful. And then he said, I think that is enough about Cosmos, but it is perhaps worth adding one thing in conclusion, and that is that, as it happens, the profoundest part of the

Christian doctrine about God, namely the doctrine of the Trinity, seems already to be implied even in Genesis. For when God created the heaven and the earth, we read that *the Spirit of God moved upon the face of the waters.* And *God said, Let there be light; and there was light.* Here the Creator, the Word, and the Spirit seem to be united in a single act.

Phlegon asked if that was the reason why Jesus, the Son of God, was called the Word.

Patrobas at once observed that the text in St. John's first Epistle which says that *there are three that bear witness in heaven, Father, Word, and Spirit,* was a late insertion, and he appealed to Philologus as to whether this was not so.

Most certainly it is, said Philologus, but that of course does not alter the fact that the Son and the Word are the same. The first sentence of St. John's Gospel undoubtedly refers to the Son. *In the beginning was the Word, and the Word was with God, and the Word was God.*

But what is the sense of calling Jesus Christ the Word? Phlegon asked.

I suppose it is like this, Philologus answered. Words are the best means that men have by which to communicate with one another, and convey their knowledge and their thought to one another. And so, when God conveys his knowledge and his thoughts to men, either by the Moral Law or the Prophets or the works of Nature, we call that the Word of God. As he has conveyed so much knowledge and so many thoughts to us through Jesus Christ, and particularly knowledge and thoughts about himself, far above anything else we learn to know and think, it is natural enough to call Jesus Christ *the* Word. And there's another point. While we are spiritual enough to be able to know and think about God, we are also carnal, that is to say, we have bodies, so that we can only know and think through the body and the senses. And so Jesus Christ the Word came to us in bodily form, which is what makes St. Paul say that *In him dwelleth all the fullness of the Godhead bodily.* A great part of that fullness bodily was exhibited in speech, and all Christ's words were words from God. And so St. John says: *The Word was made flesh and dwelt among us, and we beheld his glory as of the only-begotten of the Father, full of grace and truth.*

Is that the doctrine of the Atonement? asked Asyncritus.

No, it is not, said Philologus. It is the doctrine of the Incarnation, or the Enfleshment, as you might say. God takes

79

our manhood into himself and appears in human form, an event historical, but impossible to explain at all completely.

But at any rate an event which would be clearer, old Nereus observed quietly, in proportion as we have a clear idea of what this human nature of ours, which God took upon him, is. What does the New Testament say about that?

A big subject, Philologus replied, and we must not shirk it. And in the first place, the New Testament, and indeed the whole Bible, takes it for granted that it is man that matters. It is easy for biologists and astronomers to say that the inhabitants of this insignificant planet are an almost wholly negligible phenomenon in this mighty universe, or even that what we call Life is an unfortunate accident in the history of Matter, which had far better revert to a condition inanimate and measurable. But it is impossible to act as if that were so, and the Bible wastes no time over it. It agrees with the Greek thinker Protagoras that Man is the Measure of all Things, though not quite in his sense.

Never mind about Protagoras, Nereus said. In what sense do *you* think that Man is the measure of all things, and that it is Man that matters?

I suppose it is just this, that man puts particular values on different things, and that determines their true place in the scale of values. You wouldn't, for example, think that men merely feel pleasure from some sensations and pain from others. They do more. They value most pleasures and some pains, and call them good. They call most pains and many pleasures bad, and they resist them.

Certainly, said Nereus.

And among pleasures they rate some more highly than others.

Naturally.

And they think some kinds of pleasure are higher than some other kinds, as for example that pleasure from craftsmanship is higher than pleasure from eating.

Yes.

A clockmaker, for instance, would get more pleasure from his craft probably than from his breakfast. At least he ought to. He should get satisfaction from his skill, and some would get more still from the prospect of providing for their family or becoming famous, I dare say. The famous clockmaker Tompion may have hoped that he would be buried in Westminster Abbey.

And was he?

Yes, he was. But, continued Philologus, whatever satisfaction is to be had from fame, I suppose a still greater satisfaction may be had from love. The great Duke of Marlborough, to judge from his letters, got more satisfaction out of his home life than out of all his victories.

Yes, Love is a great thing, assented Nereus.

And the best thing of all perhaps, added Patrobas, is the Vision of God. For that is the life of man, as Irenaeus remarked nearly eighteen hundred years ago.

Well, said Philologus, I think all this gives some sense to the notion that man is the measure of all things. His values depend upon his own make-up. The world around him to some extent shapes, but is much more shaped by, the nature, or person, or spirit, or whatever you call it, that is within him.

And that, said Nereus, brings us back to where we were before. And I ask again: What does the New Testament say about human nature?

I don't really know where to begin to answer you, Philologus said. The New Testament certainly draws a very complicated picture of man's interior life, but then of course man is very complicated, much more so, I suppose, than he was ever intended to be. But just as when we have many arguments to prove a point we often content ourselves with three of them, so the New Testament contents itself roughly with the division of man's nature into Body, Soul and Spirit. Each of these brings him a different kind of satisfaction or sense of value, the Body giving the lower kinds of satisfaction and the Spirit the highest kinds. But it is just at this point that the Greek words for Body, Soul and Spirit, and their history, become so interesting.

Tell us, said Phlegon.

Then we must begin with Body, and that's not very difficult to deal with. The Greek word is *sōma*, derivation unknown, and with no ordinary English words derived from it. In Homer, who is the earliest Greek author whose works we possess, it is said to mean a corpse, and not a living body, but it comes to be used almost exactly as our word Body is. It means the material, physical man, woman or child, alive or dead. It can be used as equivalent to the word Person, and was used in particular for slaves. To the Greeks a slave was a ' body ' and no more, a significant sidelight on slavery. Any physical object can be called a body. We speak of the heavenly

81

bodies because they did. So the word Body need not cause us much trouble. The important thing is that it is connected with or contrasted with Soul.

'Keeping Body and Soul together', Phlegon murmured.

Exactly, and for the moment we will keep Body and Soul together, and keep Spirit out of it altogether. Otherwise we shall soon get confused as we do by the English words Soul and Spirit often being used loosely for the same thing or for some part of each other.

And is it the same in Greek?

Unfortunately it is, and perhaps particularly so in the Greek Testament. The two words there are *Psyche*, from which we get 'psychic', and *Pneuma* from which we get 'pneumatic'. But let us stick to Psyche for a bit.

Cupid and Psyche?

Not so fast. Psyche by itself first. It means that part of man which makes and keeps him alive. It is his animal nature, but it is more, because his life is a great deal better than that of an animal. All the things he does that show he is alive might be said to be due to his Psyche.

Then Soul isn't really quite the same as Psyche, is it?

No, Soul is rather a tiresome word, it means more and it means less than Psyche, and that is the reason, no doubt, why in recent years people have written and talked a lot about 'the Psyche' in English, when they mean the part of you that accounts for your acts and your behaviour.

And is that how the New Testament used it?

Up to a certain point. It is said to be derived from a word that means 'to cool by breathing upon', and to be trying to describe the soul as 'breath'. And that is rather awkward, because in that case it contains very much the same idea as Pneuma. You call a tyre a pneumatic tyre when you can blow air into it. On the other hand Psyche is a convenient word, because it expresses the Hebrew as well as the Greek notion of Life. You remember in the story of the Creation how man came alive: *God formed man of the dust of the ground* (that made his *sōma,*) *and breathed into his nostrils the breath of life* (that made his *Psyche*) *and man became a living soul.* That's the real basic idea of soul, as you might say. But with the animal life there comes man's adaptability and the powers of contrivance, of which he has so much more than the beasts. And at a stage a little higher still in his life you find him capable, not only of making houses and furniture and implements for himself, but of making works of art. He makes not only chairs but thrones, he not only invents words but *musical tunes* and *verses*, and finds a great satisfaction in them. And at this point we begin to wonder whether it is his Soul or his Spirit, his Psyche or his Pneuma, which is at work. The Jews just before the Christian era assigned Art and Science to a Spirit of Wisdom which filled the world, and this Spirit of Wisdom was the Spirit of the Lord. When the Christian Church came into being, it went a stage further and its members perceived this Spirit working for and in men at a higher level than art, conveying the knowledge of God as a Father and Redeemer, and enabling men to offer God a seemly worship and to know who it was to whom their worship was being offered. *God is a spirit, and they that worship him must worship him in spirit and in truth.* And the Spirit which enabled men to worship in spirit and in truth was a Holy Spirit, different from any spirit they had known. It would have been well if the Christian had used the word Soul for the visible and outward signs of life in men, such as indicate intention or happiness or passion, and had left the word Spirit to apply to the invisible life of prayer and contemplation and endurance and contentment and the like.

But are not happiness and contentment much the same thing? Phlegon asked.

Well, perhaps they are, said Philologus. But I had in mind that you can generally tell whether a person is happy, whereas you may have no idea whether he is contented. But I dare say the distinction I have in mind there is plainer to me than to you. It may be that I mean satisfied rather than contented. In any case the Christians have not used the words Soul and Spirit to emphasise respectively what is more visible and what is less visible in man's interior life. In ordinary usage the Spirit means the highest part of the Soul, but the Soul on the other hand may include all the life of man that is not purely physical, and therefore covers activities of the Spirit as well as a good deal else. In other passages, however, the distinction is clear enough. With the text from Genesis in his mind, which I was quoting just now, St. Paul says that *the first Adam was made a living soul; but the last Adam a life-giving spirit.* And since the New Testament is mainly concerned with this life-giving and with the highest man can be or achieve, its concern is mainly with the Spirit. I believe I am right in saying that in the Old Testament—that

83

is to say in the Old Testament in Greek, the word Psyche occurs something like three times as often as the word Pneuma, whereas in the New Testament it is just the other way round. There I should say that Psyche occurs about 150 times, but Pneuma close on 400 times. Their relative importance is already implied in one of St. Paul's earliest epistles—First Thessalonians —where he says *I pray your whole spirit and soul and body be preserved blameless unto the coming of our Lord Jesus Christ.*

But I have an idea, Patrobas said almost interrupting, that Psyche in the New Testament is sometimes a bad part of us.

Yes, said Philologus, one effect of exalting the Spirit is to depress the Soul, and the word Psyche comes to apply in places to the animal part of man, almost suggesting something sub-human. In particular the adjective psychic occurs always in a deprecating sense. Hermes, he said, go and look it up.

Hermes and Hermas both ran off again. Bring the book with you, Philologus called after them. And meanwhile the sun having moved round somewhat, the whole party of us got up and shifted the chairs and garden seats round so as to be in the shade. Consequently we had a view of the Victoria Tower at the Houses of Parliament laced with tubular scaffolding to the very top of the flag-pole.

What is all that for? Phlegon asked, but before anyone answered, Hermes and Hermas were back with the Concordance. Philologus asked Patrobas to tell us what it said.

Psyche occurs in five places, Patrobas said. First of all near the beginning of the First Epistle to the Corinthians. *The natural man*—'the psychic man' it says—*receiveth not the things of the spirit*—that is of the pneuma—*of God.* Then in two verses of the great chapter on the resurrection in the same Epistle it speaks of *a natural body*—the one we have now—and *a spiritual body*—the one we shall have hereafter, a rather different kind of idea from what we have been considering. Then St. James calls a certain wrong kind of wisdom *earthly, animal, devilish,* or to translate more closely ' of the earth, psychic, demonioid '.

Demonioid? asked Hermas.

Yes, that is the word in the Greek meaning ' of the same kind as a demon ', say demoniacal, if you like. And the word for earthly, by the way, generally applied to a land animal.

Then the whole thing suggests a demoniacal land animal,

Phlegon pondered. I don't know if that is how St. James thought of the human species.

Well, James was rather ferocious, Philologus said. But let us go on to the last place where 'psychic' occurs. It is in Jude. He says that certain wicked people who separate themselves are *animal, not having the Spirit*, psychic, the Greek says, not having Pneuma.

I see what it is, said Phlegon. Psyche, when contrasted with Pneuma, is the animal part of man, but when contrasted with Body or Death it may be all of man that is not Body. And Pneuma in any case is the part of man which the animals have not got.

Ah, observed Philologus, how familiar we are getting with the Greek, talking so easily, and I think pretty correctly, of Psyche and Pneuma!

And of Sōma too, added Phlegon. For I want to ask you something, he went on. When a man dies, his Sōma no doubt returns to the dust it came from, but is it Psyche or Pneuma that survives, and if only Pneuma, what becomes of Psyche?

Not a very simple question, Philologus replied. The Greeks were inclined to think that the Psyche fluttered round the tomb; and do you know that the Psyche appears to be the only word they had for a butterfly? But they also thought that the soul went a long journey and was purified, but after it was purified, even Plato's myth in the *Republic* could not do any better for it than let it enter another body.

Do the Christians believe that too? Hermes asked.

No, that is the doctrine of Transmigration. It is taught in some Eastern religions, but it is no part of Christian belief. The Christians believe that God's plan for them is that the spiritual part of them, the Pneuma, will survive and inherit an immortal life. But that does not mean that we believe in disembodied spirits. There are no ghosts in Christianity, but we shall be *clothed upon* with that spiritual body which St. Paul spoke of. *This mortality must put on immortality. It is sown a natural* or psychic *body, it is raised a spiritual body,* by which I suppose he means a body fit for the spirit, and not at war with it, as the natural body is.

A god-like destiny, said Phlegon.

A god-like destiny indeed. And of course, if the spirit is going to be immortal, it is immortal already. For it death is only a physical incident, and not a disaster or the end. And it is with this immortal spirit now and hereafter that the New

85

Testament is concerned. Look about you at that great Tower and that great Abbey, and know that they must one day be in ruins, be dissolved, but we shall be *saved*. We are not such stuff as dreams are made of.

I don't believe all that, Phlegon objected. Of course we should like to survive, but I don't see any signs that we do. I think Shakespeare was right, and that

Our little life is rounded with a sleep.

And what did he mean by that? Asyncritus asked.

He meant that life begins and ends with oblivion, I suppose, said Phlegon. Once we were not, and once again we shall not be.

To be or not to be, Philologus quoted. That is the question. And I am only telling you what answer the Apostles gave to that question, and it is the answer which the Christian Church still gives to it. It is the answer which Plato gave too, for the matter of that, without any help from the Christian revelation. In the *Phaedo* he argued powerfully, though perhaps indecisively, for the survival of the soul.

Does he make the same distinction between Psyche and Pneuma? Phlegon wanted to know.

But before Philologus had answered, Patrobas asked leave to interrupt, and then said he thought Plato meant the same by Psyche that the Greek Testament means. He thought the place that proved it was in the *Cratylus*.

What is it? queried Philologus. I don't know the *Cratylus* very well.

Why, he describes the Psyche by saying that 'when it is present with the body it is the cause of its being alive, affording it the power to breathe and renewing it. And when its power to renew the body fails, the body fails too and comes to an end'. It is in fact what makes and keeps a man alive.

And what does Plato say about the Pneuma? Phlegon asked.

Nothing at all, Patrobas answered. He uses the word, but only of the wind. With him the soul survives, but it obviously includes what we call the spirit. For in his myth of the two-horsed chariot of the soul in the *Phaedrus*, one of the horses is always soaring upwards, and the other downwards. The horses would be called Pneuma and Psyche in the Greek Testament. Plato thinks the soul is purified after it has been

86

released from the body, and what would be left after the puri-
fication is what we should call Spirit.

Well, let us call the best part of Man his Spirit, said Philologus, and agree that if any part survives it is that part. It
seems to me that in doing so we shall be true to the mind of
both Plato and St. Paul.

But what about evil spirits? suggested Asyncritus. How
do they come in?

Not very happily, replied Philologus. It was a notion of
the Jews to account for the existence of evil. But they perhaps took a false step in picturing men possessed with evil
spirits;—a vivid picture, certainly, but it includes no satisfactory account of the origin of these spirits. The problem of
evil was not well stated in these terms, and we must just put
it on one side. Let us think only of man's immortal spirit,
and suppose that he derives it from the spirit of God. This is
the sense in which he is made in God's image.

But in what sense really can you say that he was made in
God's image? Phlegon asked.

He is the son of God, Philologus replied.

A mystical and most mysterious utterance, remarked
Phlegon, but does it mean anything?

Yes, it means a lot. But in order to know what it means
you must learn another word out of the Greek Testament.

What word is that?

The word I have in mind is the word for Adoption. But
first perhaps we had better take the word Son, Philologus went
on. If I spell out the Greek letters for the word Son it looks
rather odd, HUIOS, but when you say it, it simply sounds
like Why-oss with plenty of H at the beginning.

Is that the way the Greeks pronounced it? Hermas
asked.

Not a bit, but the tradition always was, until lately, to
pronounce Greek and Latin as though they were English, as
near as you could, and I always do it still. It seems quite
sensible.

But what do other people do?

Some use what is called a 'reformed' pronunciation. I
did myself for a time, and a pupil of mine was once congratu-
lated by the then Professor of Greek at Oxford on his German
pronunciation of Greek, though what merit there could be in
that I don't really know. But anyway, Pericles certainly
wouldn't understand the way they say it at Westminster School.

The custom used to be for every European nation to pronounce the classical languages as if they were their own language. Let's do it.

Right, said Phlegon. Why-oss, a Son.

Yes, spelt in the back of your mind HUIOS. And from it comes the word translated Adoption, which really means, you might say, the Appointment of a Son. And we must have another Greek word in mind too, the word *Teknon*, usually best translated a Child. You may say that *Teknon* simply implies offspring, whereas *Huios* carries with it some sense of standing or privilege derived from the Father. I suppose there is really something of the same distinction between the English words Child and Son, and would be more still, if with us, as in the ancient world, a Son counted for ever so much more than a Daughter. We feel, or we feel that we ought to feel, that all our children are equally important, but Greeks and Jews alike felt far more about their sons than their daughters, so for them Son is a much grander word than Child, as grand perhaps as when we say Son and Heir. In fact there is a passage in St. Paul which makes me think that that is just how it was. For writing to the Galatians of the effect of their becoming Christians he says: *Thou art no more a servant, but a son; and if a son, then an heir of God through Christ.*

You'll excuse me saying so, Patrobas interjected, but I don't know if that will do, because in the Epistle to the Romans Paul does not say We are sons and therefore heirs, he says *We are children of God, And if children, then heirs. Teknon* is the word he uses there, and not *huios.*

Yes, I mustn't press it, Philologus allowed, because there usually is a definite distinction in the use of the two Greek words, much more, I think, than between Son and Child in English. Taking Son to represent Huios and Child to represent Teknon, it is rather curious to find that, while in English we don't talk about Sons and Heirs in the plural, so the New Testament never talks about children of God except in the plural. It talks enough of the Son of God, but not (like the Catechism) of a Child of God. So it follows that Jesus Christ is called the Son of God, but never the Child of God, and when we come to St. John, he never calls men the sons of God but only the children of God. And the people he is writing to in his epistles he calls his children, but he never calls them his sons. It seems that child is too poor a word to use of Jesus Christ, and because he is the Son and the only-begotten Son of the Father at that, Son becomes too grand a word to use of men.

By now Phlegon was getting impatient. What has all this to do with what? he asked rather incoherently.

A reasonable question, Philologus answered. And I think I must confess that I am sorry for all these refinements. But I am hoping they may help to show what you might mean by saying that you or Patrobas or Nereus or any other Christian is a son of God.

Of course you would mean that God is our Father, Phlegon said.

Yes, but you might say that and mean several different things. When Isaiah makes the Gentiles say to God in prophetic strain, *Doubtless thou art our father*, it does not mean the same as the centurion at the Cross meant, when he said *Truly this man was the Son of God*.

What did the centurion mean? asked Hermas. I always thought it wonderful that he saw the truth like that.

But quite possibly he didn't see the truth you think he saw, Patrobas explained. A reputable commentary—Alfred Plummer on *St. Luke*—says that perhaps he did not mean much. Perhaps he only meant 'Well, he was a hero'. You see, both Greeks and Romans, at an early stage, thought of their heroes like Hercules and Romulus as children of a god or goddess. And in the first century A.D. the expression had been given a new turn, because the first Roman Emperor had come already to be called divine—he was *Divus Augustus;* and his predecessor Julius Caesar was *Divus Julius*. So the reigning emperor Tiberius, being Augustus's successor, was the son of a divine being, that is, he was son of a god.

Well, that sounds to me rather far-fetched, Phlegon objected. But I grant you that the Jews had got hold of the idea that God was a father to Israel, and the Israelites are his sons. And they even thought they were meant to be gods themselves, as it says in the Psalms, you remember: *I said ye are gods, and ye are all the children of the most highest*. But the question is, What did the Christians make of the idea?

Why, of course they made a tremendous addition to it, answered Philologus, because they asserted that Jesus Christ was in very truth the Son of God, and that in consequence the Christians could be sons of God too by adoption. And I think it is Paul's own idea. In both Galatians and Romans, in the places we were talking about, he says we can become sons of

89

God by adoption, and if sons, then heirs. Now the Jews had thought almost exclusively of being sons of God by physical descent from Abraham, and heirs by a covenant or legal contract. But Paul said that if anyone had the confidence to become one of the family and throw in his lot with Jesus Christ, then God was ready to adopt him.

And didn't the Jews think anything like that? Phlegon asked.

No, they never thought anything about adoption. They attached enormous importance to having children, and if they were childless you can easily see in the Old Testament that they thought it a great misfortune inflicted upon them by God, for which adoption would be no proper cure. They never dreamt of adoption.

Then presumably the idea is Greek?

No, in fact it is Roman. It was fully provided for in Roman Law, and constantly resorted to. Julius Caesar adopted Augustus, and Augustus adopted Tiberius. The Greeks did sometimes practise adoption, but they do not seem to have talked about it. They only seem to have the word in inscriptions. It was like the word Relict which people used to put on widows' tombstones in this country at one time, but it was not used in ordinary life. St. Paul, however, introduces adoption into his Epistles quite often. It has even been said that it was he who introduced it into Greek literature, meaning by literature proper writings and not just inscriptions. Here, give me the Concordance. Philologus held out a hand.

Hermas handed it over, and Philologus found the place and examined it for a moment or two. Yes, here it is, he said. Paul writes of adoption five times, three times in Romans, and once each in Galatians and Ephesians. It must have sounded rather novel when the Epistles were read out, and he had in fact something new to say. First of all he names Adoption by God as one of the privileges of the Israelites, as much as to say that when they talked about Israel as God's son, adoption was what they were getting at. But the reality of adoption he claims for the disciples of Christ. . . They *have received the Spirit of adoption.* God has *predestinated them to adoption through Jesus Christ,* and in one place the Adoption is defined as *the Redemption of our body.* And by that he means that whereas because of the flesh we were slaves to sin, we now have our freedom bought for us, Jesus Christ paying the price and making us sons of the house.

Yes, that may be what he has in mind, Phlegon assented, but how does it happen?

I suppose, Philologus answered, by our becoming like Jesus Christ through living in a family or community where they are all trying to imitate him, and by being taught by the Father of the family how to do it, and that amounts to being adopted. As a matter of fact I believe quite a lot of what the New Testament means about sons and children and adoption becomes clearer if you suppose that St. Paul was trying to express the same idea that we have when we talk about one person 'taking after' another. The Greeks, as far as I know, had no corresponding word or expression, and perhaps they had not the notion of taking after one another. They must have seen family likenesses, I imagine, but they didn't think they signified. But very often the idea seems to make more of a reality of adoption and sonship as they occur in the Greek, which is useful, because adoption is not very familiar to us in this country so far, while 'taking after' is a commonplace. But anyway it all comes to this in the New Testament. We are children of Nature, natural products, but we are more, and the fact of our possessing spirit as well as body and soul makes it possible for us to take after God, and this possibility is realised by the imitation of Jesus Christ and by catching his spirit. For the fact of being like Jesus Christ is, so far as we achieve it, a taking after God, and that makes us sons of God by adoption.

There now, said Phlegon, and all the time you have never told us what the Greek word for Adoption is.

No more I have, said Philologus. It's this tiresome old word HUIOS again. Try and say Whyothessia, HUIO-THESIA, and you have it.

Phlegon pronounced the word. I have it, he said.

Well, in fact you have not, said Philologus. It does not rhyme with anaesthesia, because it has quite a different derivation and a short E—Whyothessia.

Phlegon tried again, and this time he had it. And now the company fell to musing for a while, and then Asyncritus, who had been silent for some time, said, How can anyone be a Son of God? He would be a god himself. I remember it in the Psalms, *I said, ye are gods, and ye are all the children of the most highest.*

Exactly what I quoted just now, Philologus protested.

Oh, I am so sorry, Asyncritus said. I'm afraid I wasn't

attending if you did. I've been thinking on my own about Fathers and Sons, and wondering if this father-and-son relation really helps at all in theology, or rather whether it doesn't hinder more than help.

If you mean practical theology, Nereus said, I suppose that a very great number of people would say that to begin the Lord's Prayer with *Our Father* helps a lot, and has greatly strengthened the hold it has on them. If it began with Almighty God who art in heaven I do not think there would be anything like the same feeling about it. But if you mean that to call Jesus Christ the Son of the Father does not explain anything much or make Christianity easier to believe, I rather agree with you. But I don't think I ever felt the need for explanation, perhaps not as much as I ought to have.

But I do feel the need very much, Asyncritus said. As a Christian I understand I am to worship God the Father, God the Son, and God the Holy Ghost, and this is for me as much as to say I must worship an unknown God.

Nereus appealed to Philologus. Philologus, dear friend, he said, come to the rescue.

You seem to be asking me to explain the doctrine of the Trinity, Philologus replied, and so I will if I can, but only on the strict condition that you will bear in mind that, although it is certainly the business of theology to explain things, explanations can never replace personal faith, they can only enhance it. I can't bear that line of a hymn which says 'Faith believes nor questions how'. But all the same the answers to questions in theology only satisfy the theological part of you, and there are plenty of other parts of you that have to be called into activity, if you are to come at all near being a Christian. But the doctrine of the Trinity is a very satisfying explanation for the theologically minded—which is, however, just what a good many of us are not. Still, here goes for a little lecture with questions at the end.

But here Philologus hesitated. It is not at all easy, and I want to get it right. I think I will just go round to my house and get a note-book with a paper in it which I am going to read at a theological college in a few days. I know you are not really theological students, but as I always take it for granted, when I read a paper, that my audience are not very clever— it is the best policy, I hasten to add, even when they are—I believe I have made it as clear as I can, but I don't know how clear that is, and I should be very glad to try it out on you.

Philologus lives in the Precincts quite close at hand, and while he was gone, Julia went into her house and fetched some olives and some dried figs, and we sat round and ate them, as I dare say Phaedrus and Socrates did under their plane tree long ago. Now it is difficult to eat olives and dried figs and talk at the same time, so we said nothing, and very soon Philologus came back with his paper.

All the time I had been reporting this discussion to Canon Lomax he had listened most attentively without saying a word. But now he interrupted my recital and said, I imagine you will only give a summary of Philologus's dissertation on the Trinity. So I had to tell him that as a matter of fact I had what he called the dissertation in my pocket, because I had borrowed it overnight and was meaning to return it on my way home. So I can tell you what I remember, or read it out, just as you like, I said. But I think perhaps it would be only fair to read it out, because I might easily go wrong over all this.

Quite so, agreed the Canon. Read it out then.

Philologus started by saying that his paper was called *Person and Substance*, but that need not alarm them, and he went on as follows:

'Christian theology asserts that Jesus Christ, the Son of God, took our flesh upon him, and became Man. He is both God and Man. And the question soon arose in the minds of some Christian thinkers as to how the relation between God the Father and God the Son could be expressed. And as it came to be learnt by experience that the Holy Ghost was God also, the wider question arose too, as to what could be the relation between the Father, the Son, and the Holy Ghost, seeing that they all three were God, and yet there was only one God.

'The answer to this question is that in the Trinity there are Three Persons in One Substance, and it has been said that "The Trinity is the one theological question of absolutely fundamental importance which has ever been pressed to a positive and satisfactory answer". Of those who cannot find satisfaction in it, it must perhaps be said that they are not theologically minded. But they need not be distressed by that. As old Daniel Waterland said, "It is one thing to understand the *doctrine*, and quite another to be master of the *controversy*." But without aspiring to be masters of the controversy, we might all get some satisfaction from understanding the doctrine, and if so, we ought to know at least something of what Three Persons in One Substance was supposed to mean, when it was accepted by the Church. It was Tertullian in the early part of the third century who first suggested the appropriate terms, though he did not get them quite right. He was, as it happens, the first person to make use of the notion of a Trinity (or Triad), not however in reference to God, but to Body, Soul, and Spirit. For what we now call the Trinity he began by using the terms Economy or Dispensation, as being the way in which God was pleased to present himself to the mind of man. But this was too indefinite, and too little about God as he is in himself. And after a time he got on to another line of approach. He was an African lawyer at Rome, who wrote and thought in Latin, but he was familiar with the terms of Greek philosophy and Greek-thinking Christianity. To him, thus equipped, it seemed that, if the Father was God and the Son was God and the Holy Spirit was God, it must be because they shared one Substantia or one Substance, but if they were at the same time distinct from one another, it must be because each was a Persona or Person. Tertullian never actually called the Trinity Three Persons in one Substance, but he put the theologians on the track. Chief among these were Dionysius of Alexandria and Dionysius of Rome, who engaged in a long correspondence and more or less defined the terms, and the so-called Cappadocian Fathers, Gregory of Nazianzum, Basil of Caesarea, and Gregory of Nyssa.

'Now we must try and see first what Tertullian meant by his terms. Substance is a very difficult word to define. It means many different things, and in particular " property " (as when we say " a man of substance "), or it means " something solid " (as when we say " he drew off the liquor and a white substance remained at the bottom "), or it means something like " reality " (as when we say " substance, not shadow "). This last was what Tertullian mostly had in mind, not without some touch of other meanings too. He might have said he was thinking of the substance and not the attributes or appearance of God. As to the word Person, in Latin it really means a " mask ", and so a character in a play (*persona dramatis*), and then a distinct individual or personage. So

94

when Tertullian used Substance and Person of the Father, Son and Holy Spirit he was thinking of them as three separate individuals or Persons owning one Property jointly, and this Property or Substance is their own Reality as God, in fact their Godhead. In expounding this view of the Trinity Tertullian used other terms such as status, condition, degree, species, but it was on these two words, Person and Substance, when they had been translated into Greek, that the discussion of the doctrine turned.

'And now we must see how these words were put into Greek. The Latin word Substantia was represented by two different words, Hypostasis and Ousia. Hypo-Stasis is simply the equivalent of Sub-Stantia, and both are transferred directly into English when we speak of Sub-Stance, the notion of standing or subsisting beneath. The Greek word varies in meaning quite as much as the Latin and English. It is used in the Septuagint to represent at least a dozen different words in the Hebrew. Ousia is a much simpler word. It is the abstract noun from the Greek verb for "to be", and therefore means Being. And now for the word Person. That was translated literally into the Greek Prosōpon which, like Persona, means a mask and a character in a play, and an individual, but it had about it, more than the Latin has, a notion of Personification. So Tertullian turned into Greek would seem to teach or at least to imply, that there are three Persons or individuals in one Substance or Being, and by Substance was meant something like we mean by "real existence". So we may say that the Greek did represent the Latin very fairly.

'But, as the Greek Fathers discussed the truth of this by correspondence and in conference, they found they could never agree, until they came to perceive that the word Person, or Prosōpon as they called it, was a very slippery word, and was always introducing some sort of a misunderstanding, just as the word Democracy does in our own time. And so at last they threw it out, and for it they substituted Hypostasis, leaving Ousia for the other term of the definition. It may seem strange that they could do this, seeing that Hypostasis and Ousia were supposed to be synonyms, and to be perfectly distinct from Prosōpon. But in fact in the course of the discussion the theologians, as Bethune-Baker says, had come to a kind of "agreement to use the word Hypostasis always of the special characteristics and individual existence of each Person of the Trinity, and to keep Ousia to express the very

95

being or essence of the Godhead ". This made it easy, or at least not difficult, to arrive at the formula Three Hypostases in one Ousia, or Three Existences in one Being. And this is the orthodox doctrine which theologians so much admire.

'Three comments may be added. First, the terms that were finally agreed upon, Hypostasis and Ousia, were at first regarded as meaning the same thing, and really both imply no more than Being. So the truth is that, although we can apply different epithets to God, as for example we can say that he is holy or almighty or everlasting, we can only define him in terms of existence, and say Three Beings in one Being, which is no more than what Moses taught, when he said that God called himself *I am what I am*. Secondly, note that, although the word Hypostasis took the place of Prosōpon in the Greek, the word Person has been retained in English to represent Hypostasis. We speak of Three Persons in one Substance. We should perhaps have been more exact, though perhaps not much clearer, if we had decided to say Three Substances in One Essence—Essentia from which we get Essence being the Greek word Ousia turned back into Latin for the purpose of philosophy and theology. Thirdly, note that Tertullian carefully avoided using the word Nature, and we had better do so too in discussing the Trinity, though in discussing the Incarnation it is almost indispensable.'

This was the end of the paper. Phew! said Phlegon, I don't think I can be theologically minded. It doesn't seem to me we are any further on than when we started. But Patrobas said he thought it was interesting, and Julia said it was nice, and Nereus said that it was all new to him, and he was too old to be any good at taking in new things, but he thought he might get something out of it, if he could hear it again or read it over.

Well, perhaps it might do the same for me, if I got used to it, Phlegon said. But what I should like to know is whether the words Ousia and Hypostasis occur in the Greek Testament, and if so, what they mean there.

I can tell you that out of my head, volunteered Philologus, because I went into it carefully. Hypostasis is used three times for the ' solid grounds' for something, and is adequately translated by ' confidence'. But it is used in two passages of Hebrews which are much more instructive. One is the well-known definition of what Faith is—*Faith is the substance of*

96

things hoped for, the evidence of things not seen, where
obviously Substance and Evidence both point to the solid
ground behind hope or imagination. It is substance as contrasted with shadow. And the only other passage is at the
very beginning of Hebrews, where the Son is said to be *the
express image of God's person,* or in the Revised Version,
the very image of his substance. The Greek word translated
image is Character, one of the very few words which are precisely the same in Greek and English, and means really 'the
impress of a seal', and the other word is Hypostasis which you
see can be equally well translated Person or Substance. The
author of Hebrews was just trying to say that Jesus Christ
bears all the marks of Godhead.—So I think we may conclude
that in the theological formula Three Hypostases in One Ousia,
hypostasis seems to be used in quite a New Testament way.

Well, that's good, said Phlegon, and what about Ousia?

That comes in only one passage of the whole Greek Testament, Philologus said, in the story of the Prodigal Son. And
there it comes twice and means Substance, but not at all in a
theological sense, but in the sense of Property. *Give me the
share of the property that falls to me,* the Prodigal said to
his father, and when his father, like King Lear, was foolish
enough to do so, *he wasted his substance with riotous living.*
It is clear that both Hypostasis and Ousia were freely used
for Property, and both came to be used for Reality or Being
at very many different stages and levels of thought and
meaning.

Rather slippery words then, said Phlegon. But Philologus
would not allow it. He said that to mean now one thing and
now another according to the context a word was used in, was
very different from meaning several things at once, as Prosōpon did when you tried to use it for Person.

And what about 'being of one substance with the Father,'
Asyncritus asked. Is Substance there Hypostasis or Ousia, or
neither, or both?

Well, said Philologus, I suppose the right answer is that it
is Ousia, but in fact 'being of one substance' is all one word
in the Greek, the adjective Homoousios, meaning, you perhaps
might say, Homogeneous in substance, though I am not
really sure you might say that without getting into difficulties.
What you may not say is Homoiousios, which would mean
'of like substance' with the Father; it must be 'of the same
substance', that is 'of one substance' with the Father. It

was this distinction which made the historian Gibbon say in his scoffing way that 'the profane of every age have derided the furious contests which the difference of a single diphthong excited'. Some were ready to be content with Homoiousios; the orthodox insisted on Homoousios.

And how is Homoousios used in the Greek Testament, asked Asyncritus.

It isn't there at all, Philologus said, and for that reason, although it was introduced into the Creed which was accepted at the Council of Nicaea in 325, it was withdrawn at the Council of Ephesus, and only finally established itself at the Council of Constantinople in 381.

Oh, bother the Councils, said Nereus. I never can get hold of them.

Well, said Philologus, I should be inclined to allow that 'being of one substance with the Father' is really a safer and more satisfactory expression than Homoousios.

Good for English, cried Hermas, but Hermes retaliated, Good for the Greek Testament. Stick to that and you can't go wrong.

Their father Patrobas looked approvingly at both of them. But Phlegon was not satisfied. If the Son Jesus Christ was of one substance with the Father, he said, I do not see how he could have been a man in any sense we know of. He could only have been a god who looked like a man.

That is certainly a difficulty and always has been, Philologus answered. It is, as you say, very natural to think of Jesus, if we worship him, as a god who for a period of years looked like a man, and on the other hand, if we consider him as a historical character, to think of him as a man who grew into a god, or as a being who was sometimes a god and sometimes a man. We fall into such ways of thinking. And the right way of thinking, the theological way, is only acquired and grows into a habit by practice.

How can you practise such a thing? Phlegon asked.

Just as you practise thinking that the earth goes round the sun, Philologus answered. Almost everything about you makes it natural to think that the sun goes round the earth, and probably twenty times a day we all of us talk as if it did, as when we say The sun is high in the sky, or The sun is going down, or The sun has gone behind a cloud. But we all know that really the earth goes round the sun, and have some idea how this happens, and how it affects the clock and

98

the seasons and the year. And we have this in mind often enough for us to come very early on in life to a state of never really thinking that the sun goes round the earth, although we often talk as if it did. And in the same way I go on still talking about Jesus of Nazareth as a man, though I know very well that he was God when he was on earth, and that he is still the Risen Master, although in heaven, and was and is and ever shall be both God and Man.

You can say all that, Phlegon replied, but *how* can it be? How can you really suppose it? I ask you that, just as, when I was told for the first time that the earth goes round the sun, I must have said, But *how* can it go round the sun?

I confess I can't explain the Incarnation as easily as I can explain the earth going round the sun, Philologus said, because the easy things to explain are measurable things, and the Incarnation is not a measurable thing. Still the truth of it can be expressed in a formal manner, and perhaps it would be best to state the truth of it in a formal manner, and then try and see what the formula means. We shall be using the same terms of Substance and Person. Jesus Christ is both God and Man: in the Incarnate Son there are 'two Substances in one Person'. And let me amplify this by quoting a semi-official document. *The Son Jesus Christ is God of the substance of the Father, begotten before the worlds, and man of the substance of his Mother, born in the world. . . . Who, although he be God and man, yet he is not two, but one Christ. . . . One altogether, not by confusion of Substance, but by unity of Person.*

Where does that come from? Hermes asked.

Out of the Athanasian Creed, Philologus answered.

And are all the words in the Greek Testament?

Well, the words of course, as they stand, are all English, but you would find words in the Greek Testament to translate them all; and the word for 'confusion' is interesting. In the Septuagint it is turned into a proper name and translates Babel. In the New Testament it is used of the uproar about Diana of the Ephesians.

Oh, I took the Athanasian Creed to be translated from a Greek author called Athanasius, said Hermes.

No, it is translated from the Latin, and I expect St. Athanasius had very little to do with it, though no doubt it teaches mostly what he taught. But the scholars think it was composed in Western Europe and in Latin.

99

But is it any use anyway? Asyncritus asked.

Yes, it is, but perhaps only when you get the right habit of mind, Philologus said. And the part I quoted certainly has a difficulty about it, because it says that Christ is one by unity of Person, and I rather fear, if we were putting it into Greek, we might have to use our old enemy Prosōpon, and not Hypostasis, and then we shouldn't know what we meant. But there is quite a different way of looking at the whole business.

What business is that? Asyncritus asked.

I ought properly to have said Problem, Philologus answered, the Problem of the Incarnation, and the way is a way suggested by St. Paul in the Epistle to the Philippians, a rather wonderful way, or at any rate based on rather a wonderful passage, the one in the second chapter of Philippians beginning *Let this mind be in you which was also in Christ Jesus.*

Why, that's the Epistle for Palm Sunday, said Hermas. *Let this mind be in you, which was also in Christ Jesus; Who, being in the form of God, thought it not robbery to be equal with God : But made himself of no reputation, and took upon him the form of a servant, and was made in the likeness of men : and being found in fashion as a man, he humbled himself, and became obedient unto death, even the death of the cross, Wherefore God also——*

That will do, Philologus said. How do you come to know it by heart?

I learnt it one Palm Sunday when we were a long time in church, Hermas said.

I dare say the time might have been worse spent, Philologus said. And what does it mean?

Well, I suppose it means that Jesus was made Man and was crucified also for us under Pontius Pilate, but I never thought much about the exact words.

Now that's just what I want to do here and now—think about the exact words, Philologus said.

Oh, good! said Patrobas.

Well, please think about the word 'robbery' first, Asyncritus broke in, for I haven't the slightest idea what could be the meaning of *He thought it not robbery to be equal with God.*

I don't wonder, said Philologus, because I don't think the translators from the Greek had much idea either. The Greek word, which is *harpagmos*, seems to occur only here and once in Plutarch, but there's no doubt it ought to mean 'an

100

act of snatching ', and so of course it might very well be used for robbery. But the margin of the Revised Version gives ' a thing to be grasped ', and what St. Paul is probably trying to say it ' a thing to be clung to ', that is, a thing not to be surrendered. So he means that Christ did not think his equality with God a thing not to be surrendered at any price, but he surrendered it and emptied himself.

Emptied himself? Asyncritus asked.

Yes, that is what it says in the Greek. ' Made himself of no reputation ' is just a paraphrase. The Revised Version has ' emptied himself ', and it is rather important, because it is part of the process by which Christ took our flesh upon himself.

But what did he empty himself of?

He emptied himself of his fullness, that is, I suppose, of his *power and riches and wisdom and*——

But Phlegon, who sings in a choral society, interrupted to complete the quotation: *And strength and honour and glory and blessing.*

Exactly, he emptied himself of all this, and became a slave.

A slave?

Yes, so it says in the Greek, or perhaps more exactly still, a bondsman.

Not just a servant?

No, but we mustn't make too much of the distinction. A slave in the ancient world was a servant, but he could not give notice, he could only run away and probably be caught again and flogged within an inch of his life. He was thoroughly under-privileged, and that is what our Lord became.

But wait, said Patrobas, you say he emptied himself of his fullness, but in Colossians you remember it says that *In him dwelleth all the fullness of the Godhead bodily.* How about that, if he emptied himself of his fullness in order to become man?

Philologus seemed quite at a loss, the only time in the whole course of this discussion, but presently he said that he thought he had been rather rash in saying that it was his fullness of which Christ emptied himself. The New Testament, he said, seems to speak of the fullness of God more than once, but it is not clear quite what it means. It seems almost to be some technical expression. Certainly, the fullness of the Godhead was seen in Christ when he was in a human body on earth, that is to say, he possessed the complete truth and goodness
101

and love that make God what he is. What he had emptied himself of was all that greatness and grandeur which belong to God and not to man, and which God in fact could be without and still be fully God, but which man could not have and still be fully man.

Patrobas expressed himself satisfied with this, and Philologus went on: What is so interesting about this passage in Philippians is that it tells you that Christ was in the *form* of God, and then took on him the *form* of a servant, and was made in the *likeness* of men, and was found in *fashion* as a man. *Form* and *fashion* and *likeness* are all different, and the difference is much plainer in the three Greek words than in the English. If in English you said something was 'in the form of a man', that would suggest that it was not really a man, and if you used the expression 'in the fashion of a man', you would think it meant behaving as a man would behave, but of the corresponding Greek words the one for form suggests that it really was a man, and the word for fashion suggests the figure or shape of a man with a kind of suggestion that there wasn't a man there really.

What are the Greek words? Phlegon asked.

The word for form is *Morphē*, from which we get, rather misleadingly, amorphous meaning shapeless, and the scientific word Morphology. And Metamorphosis too.

Didn't Ovid write a poem called Metamorphoses? Hermes asked.

Yes, Philologus said—or rather a series of poems about men and gods assuming new and different forms, as when Niobe was turned into a stone. But metamorphosis is also the word in the Greek Testament for the Transfiguration, though form rather than figure is the right word for Morphē.

And what is the other word besides Morphē?

The other word is *Schema*, which is familiar to us as Scheme, but doesn't mean what Scheme usually means.

What does it mean then?

I'll try and explain, Philologus said. But first of all let us get rid of likeness. Christ was made—or rather became—*in the likeness of men.* The Greek is *Homoioma*, but we need not bother about that. We have come across a bit of it already in Homoiousion, and it simply means Resemblance, as when Polonius agrees with Hamlet that a certain cloud looks like a camel, and a moment after that it looks like a weasel, and then like a whale. Jesus Christ on earth certainly looked like

102

a man, and by his likeness he was identified as Jesus of Nazareth, the carpenter's son. That's plain enough. But the important thing is to distinguish between taking upon him the *form* of a slave, and being found in fashion or figure as a man, to distinguish in fact between Morphē and Schema. Both words, and words derived from them, are fairly common in the Greek Testament. But without quoting the passages to you I can simply say that it is true without a doubt that schema, as I suggested just now, implied presenting a figure to the beholder with a kind of underlying thought that the object is not what it seems, while morphē implies a form in which something is embodied or contained or manifested in a way which gives a right impression of it and is perhaps inseparably connected with its existence. The distinction, it is true, is sometimes blurred, but it is really a clear one. If you had to translate into Greek Hamlet's remark to the Ghost, 'Thou comest in such a questionable shape', schema would be the word for 'shape'. But if you had to translate that other remark, 'My father in his habit as he lived! Look where he goes' you might very well use morphē for habit, habit of course meaning here his bearing. It really was Hamlet's father, as you could tell from the characteristic way of holding himself.

But it doesn't seem to me that 'shape' and 'habit' are really very different, said Phlegon.

No, they aren't necessarily, Philologus agreed, but they differ in their context. The shape is questionable, but the ghost's habit is to the life. And what I feel is that schema would be appropriate to the first and morphē to the second, though usually morphē would mean something deeper still, something which would affect the soul or the understanding.

Can you illustrate this?

Yes, I think I can. There's a place in the Epistle to the Romans where it says: *Be not conformed to this world, but be transformed by the renewing of your mind.* Here you have in the English 'conformed' and 'transformed', which a very good old scholar, Frederick Field, says is an admirable translation—and so it is. But in the Greek the first verb is a compound of schema and the second of morphē, because you feel —or rather St. Paul felt—that being conformed to the world would be mostly an external thing, a change of schema, whereas being transformed by the renewing of your mind would be an interior thing, a change of morphē.

103

Very interesting, Phlegon said with a touch of impatience, but what does all this really tell us about the Incarnation?

It seems to me to provide a way of looking at it, Philologus said. I will see if I can explain what I mean. The appearance of Jesus Christ in a human shape, *in fashion as a man* as it says, was necessary in order that we might look to him as a man like ourselves, but it was not necessary to his own Being. It was something that he took upon himself for a purpose. But the form or Morphē of a servant in which he lived on earth was something which, while perfectly human, was also essentially divine. He did not cling to the majesty of God— he was ready not to be equal with God in that. But he still retained the goodness and truth and love which are the very form of God. The Incarnation in fact was only possible because when Man is true to form, if I may put it so, then God and man are true to the same form, and it is the same form because Man is capable of service and therefore of a life of love, and God's life is nothing but a life of love and is therefore willing to serve. So in the form of a servant or slave God in Christ could and did come to serve and save us, no less God because he was a servant, no less a servant because he was God. *The Son of Man came not to be ministered unto but to minister.*

Then would you think, Patrobas asked, that the humiliation of Jesus Christ was the humility of God?

Yes, and that is part of the mystery of the Incarnation.

Then it is all a mystery after all, Phlegon said.

Yes, Philologus answered, but I always like to remember that mystery in English has sometimes been confused with mastery.

All very well, said Phlegon, but we seem after all to be back where we came from. In the Son are two Forms in One Shape, and that does not seem to be much better than two Substances in One Person.

Not better certainly, said Philologus, but different. And I think we must make one or two adjustments. Putting aside Person, as we did before, we will be content to say Two Substances in One Being, the Substances being the Godhead and the Manhood. About our second formula I am more doubtful, but I think the word Schema must go the way of Prosōpon because it is equally slippery, and I believe we must also assert that the form of a servant and the form of God in this passage of Philippians are not meant to be alternatives after all, but to coincide, and that all we can say of the Incarnation

104

on these lines is that there are two Existences in One Form, or better still, One Form in Two Existences, the Form of a Servant in a God-Man. Indeed, if we like to go further we can believe of the Trinity that there are Three Existences in One Form. And yet Form is not the right word there—best leave it at Three Existences in One Being. You cannot say anything of God except that he is.

There was a slight pause and then Patrobas said: I must say I have enjoyed all that very much.

But Asyncritus said that for his part he could make almost nothing of it. Could they not discuss something less theoretical, more practical?

I don't much like making the distinction between theoretical and practical, Philologus said. Sometimes the theoretical turns out to be very useful, is in fact indispensable, and sometimes what seems practical is of no importance at all.

Yes, of course, Asyncritus said, but what I mean is, couldn't we start from something we know about? The Crucifixion, for instance, or the Church, or Death, or something?

Well, I don't think any of us knows much about Death, and the Church is what the Christians are least agreed on. About everything else they agree in general as to what the Christian religion has actually professed to teach, though it is true that they tend to fall into two groups, those who think it wants altering, and those who think it important to keep it as it is. But as to the Church there are views in great variety, and a sect for each view, from those who think it a divine society unlike anything else in the world to those who, while they think that the Christian religion is to be practised by groups as well as by individuals, do not think these groups differ from any other groups intended to maintain causes or ideas, except that the Christian cause or system of ideas matters most. Some of these organised groups think it absolutely necessary to have bishops, some think it important but not necessary to have them, some think you may have them but only because it is convenient, and some think you certainly may not have them at all.

Then wouldn't it be a good thing to discuss what the Church really is, Phlegon suggested, or at any rate to know what the word is intended to mean?

Yes, said Philologus, that's the right idea. But unfortunately the word Church is purposely a very vague word, and its derivation is not at all certain. And what is more, if

105

we look in the New Testament we find that, while the Apostles write very frequently of and to the Church and the Churches, the Gospels use the word very infrequently.

What word? said Phlegon.

The word Church.

But what is the Greek word?

Ecclesia, from which we get the word Ecclesiastical.

Ecclesia and Church don't sound very much like one another.

No. In French and Italian and Spanish they have kept ecclesia in recognisable form—église, chiesa, and yglesia; in Welsh too, eglwys. But in English we use the Northern word church, in Scotland kirk, in Germany Kirche. It is supposed to be a corruption of the Greek *kyriakon* meaning ' the Lord's thing', but this is not certain, and even if it were, to call the Church 'the Lord's thing' is a very slender clue to its nature.

But anyway, said Hermes, you were saying that the Church is hardly ever mentioned in the Gospels, and yet my impression is that there is a great deal about the Church in the Gospels.

That, I expect, is because you have been brought up on good Church teaching, said Philologus, and so you have the impression that when the New Testament talks about the Kingdom of God it is talking about the Church.

Yes, I think I have, said Hermes. And isn't it so?

Well, I should say it is only so in a very rough and ready way, Philologus said. But look in the Concordance and see how the words Church and Kingdom do occur. And while Hermes is looking, he said to the others, let us remind ourselves that Milton wrote two fine sonnets to Cyriack Skinner. I don't know who this Skinner was, but I suppose his father must have intended to dedicate him to the Lord when he called him Cyriack.

I wonder if a girl was ever called Ecclesia, Phlegon said.

I should think there is hardly a name you could think of that some girl hasn't had, said Julia. I noticed the other day in some book or paper something about a girl whose Christian name was Cricket. But we are going off the point. Hermes, how are you getting on? she called out.

Hermes was counting steadily. And almost directly he said: Ecclesia occurs in only two verses in the Gospels, both in Matthew, nearly a hundred times in the Acts and Epistles, and twenty times in Revelation, all but one time in the first

106

three chapters, that is, in the message to the Seven Churches of Asia.

Fairly decisive, said Philologus. And what about the Kingdom?

I am afraid I don't know what the Greek word is, Hermes said. You haven't told us yet.

Nor I have, said Philologus. The word is *Basileia*, from *Basileus*, a King. Hermes began to look it up.

Hermas said, I suppose when a boy is called Basil it is the same as calling him a king.

Not quite, said Philologus. Basil is short for *Basileios* which means Royal. But the derivation has been quite forgotten. You don't in fact think of a king when you hear someone called Basil any more than when you hear someone called Roy, though I suppose the name Roy was originally given to suggest Royalty. It was so in Meredith's *Harry Richmond* anyway. And in the same way basileia, a kingdom, comes to mean any state where there is a sole governor at the head, and therefore it is suitable, or at least as suitable as any word can be, for the government of God. Well, Hermes, how does it stand this time?

Just as you said, Hermes answered. Basileia comes more than 120 times in the Gospels, only 27 times, I think, in the Acts and Epistles, and nine times in Revelation, and throughout it is almost always of the Kingdom of God or the Kingdom of Heaven.

Very well, let us take Ecclesia first then, Philologus said.

Why? Phlegon asked.

Because the Epistles were written before the Gospels.

But if we know anything at all about Jesus, Phlegon answered, he must have used the phrase 'the Kingdom of God' over and over again before any of the Epistles were written, while we can't say that he used the word Ecclesia more than two or three times, though of course he may have.

Right, said Philologus. That's a sound point, so let us take the Kingdom first and the Church after.

I believe, said Patrobas, that you will have to take them both together.

Well, I will, at any rate in the first sentence, said Philologus.

And what is your first sentence then? Phlegon said.

It is this, that Basileia and Ecclesia are both political words,

107

but the first is autocratic and the second is democratic. And as autocracy and monarchy were not very respectable in the old Greek world with its city-states where the People ruled, or thought they ruled themselves, a Basileus was not much liked, and the title, if used without qualification, meant that horrid King of Persia. But all the same it was much more respectable than the other words, Despot and Tyrant. A Basileus would generally have some sort of right to his throne, and the word was the usual one for an hereditary ruler. The fatal objection to a king as such was that his subjects had no appeal from him. They were completely in his power. But when the idea of kingship is applied to God, that objection falls away, and the kingdom or reign of God is a natural expression to imply that we are in God's hand, under his direction, subject to his laws, and the object of his care. One can hardly doubt that Jesus himself used both expressions, the Kingdom of God, and the Kingdom of Heaven. He would have found amongst his neighbours and countrymen many pious Jews who were expecting or at least hoping for the establishment of God's reign on earth, and he made use of the idea, but he preached often, it may be always, that it was not an earthly kingdom, but in heaven or within us, perhaps I should say in heaven *and* within us. And the earliest Christians caught the language and something of its meaning, though even the Apostles themselves did not easily abandon the notion of a reign of God upon earth. Certainly Saint Paul caught the idea from somewhere. *The kingdom of God is not meat and drink*, he wrote, *but righteousness and joy and peace in the Holy Ghost*. And again, *Flesh and blood cannot inherit the kingdom of God*. It is in a different world from food and drink and flesh and blood.

Then the kingdom of God is obviously not the same as the Church, Hermes said. Because the Church is in the same world as food and drink and flesh and blood.

Yes, and that is just where the Church comes in. The Church is the community here and now which is trying, you may say, to take upon itself the form, the Morphē, of the Kingdom of God. I do not think you could say it is an attempt to realise it, but rather to present it by a visible action, just as Dante in the *Paradise* does not really describe heaven, but he represents it. The Church is of course a real institution, but it is not the Kingdom of God, just as the actor is a real man, but he is not the real Hamlet.

Here Phlegon interrupted after his manner. Why is the Church called the Ecclesia anyway? he said.

Ecclesia, said Philologus, means literally 'a calling out' in the sense in which they used to talk about 'calling out the Militia', but it came to be used in the self-governing City States of Greece for the general assembly of the citizens. It excluded women, children, and slaves, but the adult male citizens could all come to the ecclesia if they liked, and in Athens their business was to discuss and vote on matters put before them by the Council or *Boulé*, an elected body of four or five hundred members. From the Greek political world the word came into the Greek Old Testament and into the vocabulary of Greek-speaking Jews as the name of the Jewish people assembled for religious purposes, what our Bible calls *the congregation of Israel*. And from there it was natural that the Christians should adopt it for their meetings, and so ecclesia was from the first the word for a Christian congregation, and later for the place in which they met, first for the Church as a community that is, and then for the Church as a building. It has really much less of a political significance than the Kingdom of God. For the Kingdom of God is certainly offered to us as an alternative to the body politic, whereas the Church, although it stands alongside of the body politic, is yet entirely distinct from it, a thing apart.

But would you be prepared to say that the Church is intended to become the Kingdom of God? Phlegon asked.

No, not the Church, Philologus said. *The kingdom of the world* is to become *the kingdom of our God and of his Christ*.

Then is the human race supposed to improve until it becomes fit to have a Kingdom of God established for it?

Well, yes and no. *The Kingdom of God cometh not with observation*. The New Testament seems to speak of it as being brought about by a catastrophe of some sort, a sudden upheaval or revolution in the fullness of the time, which I suppose means when God is ready if I may so say. It is a question whether the human race is making progress at all, but in any case it shows few signs of making progress towards the Kingdom of God. But I think you might say that the Church is the school for the Kingdom, though they are no more the same thing than Eton is the same as Lambeth Palace or the Stock Exchange. And perhaps I might usefully elaborate this parallel. Eton can prepare a boy to be a successful Archbishop of Canterbury or a successful stock-broker, but
109

it doesn't profess to teach him how to be an Archbishop or a stock-broker. Similarly the Church prepares you for a life with God, though you are not living with God while you are in it. It was Dante's idea in fact that, if we could be purified and return to a state of innocence, the Church would disappear, and it is not quite irrelevant, I suppose, to remember that Karl Marx said that when the Communist state got going, politics would wither.

Well, I wonder whether the Church is much of a success really, Asyncritus said.

Perhaps not, Philologus answered, but success is not its object. Its object is the vision of God. And to reach that end it has to be holy, catholic, apostolic, visible, indefectible and one. It may not succeed, it is the trying to be all this that matters. But as the Greek Testament never calls it catholic or apostolic or visible or indefectible, I expect we had better leave all that alone.

That seems a pity, Asyncritus said, because, while I think I have some sort of an idea what is meant by saying that the Church is holy or the Church is one (or should be), I have a very vague idea really of what is implied by its being catholic and apostolic, and I don't know at all in what sense it is called visible, and I don't even know what indefectible means. Do just tell me quickly.

Well, very quickly then, Philologus said. These are what are called the marks of the Church. It is holy because it belongs to God. It is catholic (a word specially taken over from the philosophers in the second century to describe it) if and because it is intended for the generality of mankind. The catholic church is the general church, the normal church, and if you disagree with what it teaches, you ought just to ask yourself whether it is the church that is being odd or yourself. Whether perhaps it is you that are a bit abnormal or even subnormal.

Well, that seems fair enough, Hermas said.

The Church is apostolic because it teaches what the Apostles taught, Philologus went on, and it is visible, because it consists of the whole body of baptised Christians, who have not rejected our Lord. It does not consist of a body of the 'elect' of whom it can only be said that God alone knows who they are. That won't work.

Are there no unbaptised people in the Church? Hermes asked.

110

No, Philologus said. There may be unbaptised persons for whom God will do great things, but the promises of God to his Church are for the baptised.

Well, that does not seem fair to me, Hermes said.

I can't help that, Philologus said. I believe I am telling you the truth. I know the English for the most part attach no importance to this particular doctrine, and we could probably go on arguing about it all night. But I must finish off the marks of the Church. It is indefectible, that is to say it cannot fail. *The gates of hell shall not prevail against it.* That does not mean that it is infallible. It has not by any means the appearance of being entirely preserved from error. But it is founded on the triumphant idea that God has appeared as a man to save mankind. And that truth men will never finally abandon. At times they can't believe it, but they will always come back to it.

Philologus had not in the course of the discussion spoken with so much emphasis before. And I suppose in this kind of discussion emphasis, while it impresses, also subconsciously antagonises. That remains to be seen, Phlegon murmured to Asyncritus. But no one said anything to Philologus and he continued:

And finally the Church is one. Ideally it is one great united body, in actuality this has never been so. There are signs of disunion and party strife from the start—heresy the Greeks called it, which I suppose means 'choosing'. So after all what keeps the Church together is something internal, it is the common experience of those who take Jesus Christ for their Saviour. Therein is the communion of the saints, the common spirit, the community life of the Ecclesia.

The Church of Christ is a mighty thing, Nereus said.

Yes, said Patrobas, but the Kingdom of God is greater, for it is the end. *Then cometh the end, when he shall have delivered up the Kingdom to God, even the Father.* It is fatal to make the Church an end in itself. It is a great engine which we all have to keep running sweetly, if we can. But no engine is kept running for its own sake, nor is the Church. It is the Body of Christ. It is the instrument by which he sanctifies and saves us.

I think it is very hard to say how it sanctifies and saves us, Phlegon said. You don't seem to see it doing it much, even if it is a visible Church. Though I must confess, he added, that I don't clearly know what is meant by being saved.

111

It was now close on six o'clock, and Philologus suggested that we should go into the Abbey and hear what they call the Special Choir sing anthems, then get some supper, and come back to his house and finish the discussion.

Or my house, I said.

I think my study will do best, he said, because I know where to lay my hands on my books there. Let us meet at nine o'clock.

And now let us go into the Ecclesia, said Hermas.

Yes, let us, several of us said.

When we assembled once more the evening seemed so pleasant that we went into the garden again after all. The talk was on the singing we had heard in the Abbey, and it was generally agreed that Parry's anthem *I was glad* is a very fine piece.

Yes, Philologus said, *I was glad when they said unto me: We will go into the house of the Lord. Our feet shall stand in thy gates, O Jerusalem.* I do certainly feel glad when I go into the House of the Lord, and yet I often wonder why. I really couldn't say why, though I go very often and with the greatest alacrity.

I go often, too, said Patrobas, and I suppose for the traditional reasons, to render thanks for the great benefits I have received at God's hands, to set forth his most worthy praise, to hear his most holy word, and to ask those things which are requisite and necessary as well for my body as my soul.

Yes, said Philologus, but of course to do it all corporately, otherwise you might do it at home. You join with all the rest of the congregation and with the whole Church. And yet I feel a certain unreality about it. What I love more than anything is the Cathedral kind of Evensong which they have in the Abbey, yet one doesn't have any active part in it at all.

I don't know, said Nereus reflectively. After all, the words and the music are not the whole of it, nor for the matter of that are the prayers and praises. As I look back on a long life I feel that the part of going to church that matters is its power to sanctify and save by the ministry of the Word and Sacraments, and Cathedral Evensong is a stupendous ministry of the Word. And when I speak of sanctifying and saving you may thank me for bringing you all back to where we left off before.

I do thank you, said Phlegon. For I want to know what

sanctifying and saving means. Whether going to church has that effect or not, it is the effect that is claimed for the Christian religion in general, and I should think it must be rather a difficult process, judging by the actual Christians and church-goers you see around you—I must add, including myself.

Many are called, but few are chosen, Patrobas said. All the same, when you do see a sanctified life it is very impressive, and cannot possibly be sneered at.

I don't mean to sneer, Phlegon said. But I am not at all sure that I should recognise a sanctified life if I saw it.

It means of course a life that has become holy, said Philologus. And holiness being the peculiar attribute of God, a sanctified life is a godly life, and for a Christian that can't mean anything but a life lived for God and taking for its guide the imitation of Christ.

Then a sanctified life might be a hidden life, Phlegon said.

It might, or it might not, Philologus answered. And it might be a very good life or it might not. That is according to the measure of grace. It may be good, but it must be godly, that is to say, it must take God into account, and it is hardly possible to take God into account without getting better. But this growth in grace and godliness is what is described as being saved, and that is really what we are talking about the whole time, for the whole New Testament is busy offering what it calls Salvation. One of the earliest names for Christianity was the Way, and if you had asked What way? the answer would be the Way of Salvation. And to trace the way you must look at the signposts, and the signposts are certain words in the vocabulary of the early Christians, and therefore not infrequent in the Greek Testament.

What words, for instance? Phlegon asked.

Such words as saviour, resurrection, glory, Philologus said.

Well, we know what they mean, Phlegon said.

Yes, up to a certain point, but not exactly, because, like the words we have already considered, they have a history, and the Christians chose them—in Greek—because of their history, and their history before and since is worth studying, if you really want to know what they mean properly.

Tell us about them, said Phlegon. I do want to know.

Let us begin with Saviour then, Philologus said. The Greek word is *sōtēr*, from which we get soteriology which is the science of salvation, which in Greek is *soteria*.

113

But what is salvation? Phlegon asked.

Well, I suppose it is really the state of mind in which you feel safe. Perhaps it is a mixture of social security and assurance, feeling safe from danger and ill-health and pain, and also being sure that everything will be all right in the end.

It sounds as if it was something you plan for.

No doubt people often think of it like that. They hope that legislation, if it is wise and based on knowledge, will provide security in all its varied aspects. But until modern times, although men have always had an ardent desire for security, they thought of it differently. They did not much think it was attainable in the ordinary course of history, and perhaps they were right. In the ancient world Jews and Gentiles alike fixed their hopes on the appearance of a Saviour. In fact they looked for the appearance of God himself. But the Jews got at the idea from one direction and the Greeks from another.

Then let us have the Jewish idea first, Phlegon said.

Very well. It is not necessary to go back to their earliest notions of the matter. It is enough to say that in course of time, after they became a nation and had dealings and disagreements with other nations ruled by kings, they came to think that no other than God was the king who ruled them, and although they fell away from this high and mighty idea of a theocracy as it is called, and had earthly kings beginning with Saul, they still believed in God's government of the nation, and when they were in difficulties they professed to expect that God would come himself, or send his servant, to save them and bring them the prosperity which results from the reign of a great king. In the Psalms salvation and a saviour often come to the individual, but the general idea in the Old Testament is of the nation being saved. Thus in Psalm 98 in ascribing a victory to God it says, *He hath remembered his mercy and truth toward the house of Israel: and all the ends of the world have seen the salvation of our God.* Or this in Isaiah from the famous passage about the wilderness: *Say to them that are of a fearful heart, Be strong, fear not: behold your God will come with vengeance, even God with a recompence, he will come and save you.* Or where God says, *Surely they are my people, children that will not lie. So he was their Saviour,* it says. But rather naturally this notion of God saving Israel tended to acquire a political interpretation. At the time when Jesus was born they were looking for a saviour,

114

an Anointed one, that is to say a king, who would rid them of the Roman domination. And it is important to remember that Jesus Christ means an Anointed Saviour.

Do you know, said Asyncritus, I don't know whether Jesus or Christ means Anointed. I believe I thought they both meant Saviour.

Oh no! Philologus said. Christ is the Greek for Anointed, and Jesus is the Hebrew for a Saviour, or rather the Greek form of the Hebrew name Joshua which means a Saviour. It is the same name as Joshua, and there's a tiresome place in the Epistle to the Hebrews where it says *if Jesus had given them rest,* meaning 'if Joshua had given them rest', which is very hard to guess, and there's a similar use of Jesus for Joshua in St. Stephen's speech in Acts, but it's not so difficult to guess there. The Revised Version has changed the name to Joshua in both places.

Joshua was the saviour of the Israelites in war, wasn't he? Phlegon suggested.

He was indeed. He was the military chief at the only period in their history when they were really successful in war—at their first entry into Palestine. And it may be that the Jews didn't easily think of a Saviour without some thought of Joshua.

When they thought of a Saviour then, they thought of victory.

Often enough no doubt, but not always. A pious old man like Joseph, the husband of Mary, could dream of a child being called Jesus, or rather Joshua, because he would save men from their *sins,* and the father of John Baptist had the same thought about him. *Thou, child, shalt be called the prophet of the Highest : for thou shalt go before the face of the Lord to prepare his ways; To give knowledge of salvation unto his people by the remission of their sins.* It is one of the great contributions made to religion by the Jews that the salvation you really want is to be saved from your *sins.* If you could be safe from the effects of sin you would have got a long way, they thought, and rightly.

Then the Jewish Saviour seems to be something of a God, and something of a King, and a sort of commander-in-chief, and a prophet too, or at least a preacher.

Yes, he was all that, and Jesus Christ the Anointed Saviour was certainly all that and more too.

Surely not a commander-in-chief?

Well, in the Epistle to the Hebrews he is called *the Captain of our salvation,* and the word translated 'captain' means 'chief leader'.

No, said Patrobas, the word means 'author' or 'originator'.

I know they say so, Philologus answered, but I never believed it. And in one of the two places where the word occurs in Acts, it says that God exalted Jesus to be 'a leader and a saviour'. I do not see how it can be 'an author' in that context—but anyway we can let it go, and be content for now to have got some idea of the kind of Saviour the Jews pictured to themselves.

And what about the Gentiles? Phlegon asked.

The Greeks that is. They were quite as familiar as the Jews with the notion of a Saviour. They applied the title Sōtēr to many of their chief gods, and to Zeus in particular. Then it came to be applied to princes, to Ptolemy I for example about 300 B.C., and in the first century A.D. to the Roman Emperor. An inscription speaks of Nero as 'Saviour and Benefactor of the World'.

And I recollect, Patrobas said, that when St. Paul first visited Ephesus there was an inscription there put up only a few years before, which called Julius Caesar 'God made manifest and common Saviour of mankind', which would be meant to imply that he was a god in human form intervening with power over the whole world.

That is very interesting, said Philologus. And it may have been just some idea of that sort which led all Julius Caesar's successors to call themselves 'son of god'. And Saviour also got to be quite a familiar title. But familiarity blunts the meaning of titles, and to call the sovereign a Saviour came perhaps not to mean anything very definite, any more than the title 'Royal Highness' does with us.

But what would Greek-speaking Christians in the first century mean by calling Jesus a Saviour, Phlegon asked. How would they come to do it?

It would be easy in one way, Philologus answered. They would be familiar with the word Sōtēr as a suitable title for a king, and also as a word that meant both Saviour and Healer, because in Greek the same word that means 'to save' means also 'to heal'. And as they thought of Jesus as some kind of a king and saviour and knew for a fact that he had been a healer, and also knew that the name Jesus means a saviour, it would be very natural to call him by the name Sōtēr or Saviour as soon as it occurred to them. I expect it occurred to the Jewish Christians first and the Gentiles took it over from them. In the New Testament you can see the word assuming a very solemn and glorious aspect when applied to Jesus. It occurs very infrequently in the Gospels and Acts and only in a distinctly Jewish connection. It is not in St. Paul's earlier epistles at all, but in the later ones it looks something like a title, as in the Epistle to the Philippians where it speaks of *heaven, whence we look for a Saviour, the Lord Jesus Christ,* and in the still later Epistles to Timothy and Titus and in the Second Epistle of Peter, it becames a title just as much as it is with us. By the end of the New Testament period it has quite established itself. And it was bound to in the end—in spite of the rather disagreeable connection with earthly princes—because the Gospel message was so full of the notion of being healed and saved.

Yes, but how were men going to be saved? Phlegon asked.

They had been saved already, so the earliest Christians believed, saved from disease and blindness and lameness and demons and from their sins. And there was a great deal more to come, they thought. But the great thing, as I said just now, was to be saved from their sins. That is the beginning of everything.

But what is it like when it happens? Phlegon persisted.

What? Being saved from your sins? It is to be rid of the effects of them, and as the effects of sin are unrighteousness and the wrath of God, what the sinner needs is justification by faith and reconciliation with God. And there, you see, I have uttered two great new words, Justification and Reconciliation.

Two Latin words by the sound of them, but I suppose they come from the Greek Testament. And what are the Greek words, what do they mean? What is justification by faith?

Let us take reconciliation first. The Greek for it is *catallagé* and it really means 'Exchange'. There is essentially something mutual in it. So if there is to be reconciliation between God and man, God must do something for men and man must do something for God.

But are not God and man always doing something for one another? God gives and man prays.

True. Or at any rate God is always loving man and being kind to him. But their relation (what old writers call their commerce) is not anything like it was meant to be. Man has
117

turned away from God and gone his own way, so God cannot do all he meant to do for man, any more than you can do all you would for someone you care for, if they don't care for you.

Then it looks as if reconciliation between God and man means reconciling man to God.

That is what they used to say, Philologus answered.

It was insisted on by Lightfoot and by Westcott, Patrobas said, and everyone followed them. But there is a reaction among scholars now, and they tend to emphasise that reconciliation must, as you said, be mutual.

Yes, said Phlegon. I think they are right. God's justice compels him to take a poor view of man, because the human race with its selfishness and greed is doing so poorly. Man must make a gesture.

And has man made any gesture? Phlegon asked.

In a way Yes, and in a way No. The idea is that he cannot do anything for himself. He has had the Law and no man has kept it. In fact the Law has only made things worse. Or at least that was what St. Paul thought. *Where no law is,* he said, *there is no transgression.*

But I should say there never was a time in human history when there was no law. Human society isn't possible without law.

That may be so. And in that case the law has always been broken, so reconciliation has always been a crying need, which man himself could not supply. And so God had to supply it. *He sent his Son into the world to save the world,* St. John says, and St. Paul says that *God was in Christ reconciling the world unto himself, not imputing their trespasses unto them.* And I suppose it was the sinless life of Jesus on earth that reconciled God to Man. He did not have to take such a poor view of man after all, if a man could live a life like that.

But Jesus Christ was not a typical man, Phlegon said.

But that is just what the Apostles taught that he was, Philologus answered. He was a perfect man in the sense of being what we were all meant to be. He summed up the possibilities of man, and God's intention for us is that we should *all come unto a perfect man, unto the measure of the stature of the fulness of Christ.* He was nothing that we could not be, if we were without sin.

Yes, but that is exactly it, Phlegon said rather impatiently.

As we none of us are without sin, the fact that Jesus Christ was sinless doesn't get *us* any further on with God.

Yes, but it does. It is a common experience that if you think poorly of a lot of people and then find even one of them who wins your approval, you think very differently of the whole lot. To have met a single nice person from a particular school or regiment or even from some particular country makes all the difference in the world to one's view of the school or regiment or country they belong to.

But still the life and death of Christ did not make men as a whole any better at once, so where does the reconciliation come in?

The Roman Catholics say that faith in Christ does make people better from the start and so they are justified in the sense of ' being made righteous '. And I suppose that may be true. But still you have the difficulty that God can't begin with men till they are better, and they can't be better till he does something about them. And in a way the fact of our falling so far short of what we ought to be in spite of the example of Christ makes us very poor things indeed. But there is another way of describing the situation, and that is by saying that we can't acquire any merit whatever we do, but that God is pleased, so to say, to take the will for the deed, and reckon us righteous, although we are not, if we show that we should like to be faithful disciples of Christ if we could. That is what the Protestants mean when they talk of ' justification by faith '.

And which of these two views is right, the Roman Catholic or the Protestant?

It is not very easy to say that either is wrong. But the second view seems to be supported by one of St. Paul's main contentions. There must be twenty texts at least in which he seems to say that man is reckoned righteous by God, when he is not actually righteous.

And that then is what is meant by justification?

Yes, we are on to defining justification now. Reconciliation between God and man is necessary, but there is a deadlock because man can't begin his part till he is better, and God can't make man better until he begins his part. And the deadlock is resolved by God reckoning man better, and forgetting and forgiving his past.

But that is a fiction, if he is not really better, and God cannot lie, said Phlegon.

But before we come to that, said Patrobas, we had better

119

make sure what is the real meaning of justification in the Greek Testament. What is the word for 'justify', and do we know what it means? That is what a scholar is bound to ask himself.

Yes, said Philologus, this is certainly one of the places where a knowledge of the Greek is all important.

But I told you I don't know any Greek, Asyncritus said.

Some Latin then?

Very little.

Well then, attend to me carefully. You know the Latin word Magnificat, I am sure.

Yes, it is the name of one of the canticles in the First Chapter of Luke's Gospel: *My soul doth magnify the Lord*.

Yes. Then what does Magnificat mean?

'Doth magnify' I suppose.

And what would 'fortificat' mean then?

'Doth fortify' I suppose.

And 'classificat'?

'Doth classify'.

And 'mortificat'?

'Doth mortify'.

And 'mollificat'?

'Doth mollify'.

Yes, and so you see there is a kind of Latin word, not in the great classical writers, it is true, but freely coined later on, which ends in i-c-o and corresponds to words in English which end in i-f-y, like clarify, certify, beautify and so on. These words tend to suggest making rather than doing, making clear, making certain, making beautiful, and so they are called factitive or causative verbs, just by way of finding a label for them. Now in Greek there is a similar set of these factitive verbs ending in a short o and a long ō (o—ō). There is one for example corresponding to the word clarify. And there is one which corresponds to fortify or make strong, though I seem to remember it only occurs in the Greek version of Isaiah somewhere. Still there they are, these factitive verbs in English and Latin and Greek which imply making something to be of some kind, making a fortress to be strong, for instance, fortifying it in fact.

Yes, I see that, Asyncritus said.

Now listen carefully, Philologus continued. There is a Greek verb of this kind which is formed from the Greek adjective for ' just '. It corresponds to the Latin justifico which was probably specially made to translate it, and corresponds also to the English ' justify '. I think you ought to know the sound. It is *dikaio-o*.

And from what you have said it must mean ' to make just ', or I suppose, ' to make righteous '.

Well, in fact it doesn't, and that is why I asked you to attend carefully, because it is a rule for such verbs, that, when the word from which they are formed has a physical sense you translate with the word ' make ', as ' to make blind ' or ' to make clear ', but when the adjective has a moral significance, then it means ' to reckon ', as for example ' to reckon worthy ' or ' to reckon just '. And the distinction holds good in the main for English verbs of the corresponding class too. ' Clarify ' for example means ' to make clear ', but ' vilify ' means ' to reckon vile '. The word ' magnify ' is a good illustration. Where ' great ' has a physical sense, ' to magnify ' means ' to make great ' as with what we call a magnifying glass, but where the sense is ' morally great ' it means ' reckon great ', as in the words *My soul doth magnify the Lord*, which cannot mean to say ' makes God great ' because he is already infinitely great, but it means to ascribe greatness to him, to reckon him great.

And so to justify (in Greek) means ' to reckon just '.

Yes, that is exactly where I wanted to get to.

Then having got where you wanted, said Patrobas, will you tell us whether you discovered this rule about the factitive verbs for yourself. Is it your own rule?

I would rather say that I have verified it for myself, Philologus answered. It is admirably stated by Sanday and Headlam in their commentary on the *Romans* somewhere.

I would have taken it on your authority alone, Patrobas said, but I am rather glad you have Sanday and Headlam to support you. But what you have to show next is that the word ' justify ' is in fact used like this in the Greek Testament.

It is said by good scholars that it is so with no exception. But without going through the instances, I will say first that the Septuagint constantly uses it like this. And now as to the New Testament, what about this out of St. Matthew's Gospel: *By thy words thou shalt be justified, and by thy words thou shalt be condemned.* Or this from Luke: *All the people that heard him, and all the publicans, justified God.* But of course the passages in St. Paul are the most interesting ones, because

121

he built up a great doctrine on the basis of justification, especially in the Epistle to the Romans. He says that *by the works of the law shall no flesh be justified in his sight*—that is, in God's sight. But the most striking passage is one where he virtually defines justification by faith: *To him that worketh not, but believeth on him that justifieth the ungodly, his faith is counted for righteousness.* This is his doctrine in a single sentence. It is not doing, but believing; not work, but faith, which justifies the ungodly. Of course at this point you might say that that means that believing makes the ungodly into a just man. But Paul carefully adds that his faith is credited to his account apart from works. It *is counted* to him *for righteousness.* It is *imputed* to him.

And there, Phlegon said, you come back to my point. If a man is not made righteous, God can't pretend that he is righteous.

It isn't a case of pretending, Philologus answered. When the Prodigal Son in the parable came back to his father, his father did not pretend to think he was righteous, but he acted as though he was. He forgave him because he had faith in him, and the father had faith in the son because the son had faith in him, and this put them once more in a right relation. That is where their reconciliation comes in, and the method of it is justification by faith, the son's faith in the father, but that is only possible because of the father's invincible faith in the son and his willingness to trust him again and reckon him righteous by way of a new start. And that is exactly what St. Paul felt had happened to him. He saw that the law kills because you never can keep it, whereas faith gives you a new start and, if it is faith in Christ, makes it possible to begin to try out a new and better life. And that is why he was always quoting the text out of the Old Testament: *The just shall live by faith.*

Oh! cried Phlegon. The Old Testament teaches justification by faith as well then.

No, said Philologus. It was Habakkuk who said that *the just shall live by his faith*, but he only meant that the good man by his steady perseverance would save his life, when the wicked perished—a common thought among the Jews, of which the Christian version is to be found not in justification by faith, but in the promise *He that endureth to the end the same shall be saved.* This was one of the watchwords of the earliest Christians, and St. Paul no doubt made *The just shall live by faith* another watchword, at least it is quoted in Romans, Galatians and Hebrews which suggests a fairly common use of it, though it is not quite the same use every time. But I suppose he only used it as a kind of illustration, just as we use quotations from Shakespeare. It is not an exact statement of the Christian experience. It would be truer to say that 'The justified come alive by faith'. They are as good as dead from the effects of sin, and they come *alive unto God,* before they begin to live a good life, because they accept God in Jesus Christ, and that is what we call faith. Paul often talks of being dead and being alive in that sort of way. And that is where the Resurrection comes in alongside of Reconciliation.

I can understand, Phlegon said, that the life of Christ on earth was pleasing to God, and an example to men, and that it might therefore establish better relations between God and man, but what I do not see is just where the death and resurrection of Christ come into the scheme. The resurrection is said to be the very heart of the Christian religion, and Christianity is sometimes called 'the Religion of the Resurrection'. But why exactly? Why does the death of Christ on the cross guarantee the forgiveness of sins, and why should the resurrection of Christ be an assurance of our resurrection? Might we not feel more reassured by the fact of the resurrection of Lazarus or Eutychus or Dorcas or Jairus's daughter, since they were more in our situation?

The answer to that, Philologus said, is partly suggested by considering that the Resurrection of Christ did in fact have such an effect upon the Apostles that they founded the Church, whereas the raising of Lazarus seems to have made only a brief impression, and all St. Luke could say of St. Paul's restoration of Eutychus was that the brethren *were not a little comforted.* The truth is that when we speak of the resurrection of Christ we are speaking of *The* Resurrection. The word has come to have a special and almost technical meaning, having reference not to a single event, but to a whole series of events which are inseparably connected. Jesus, after his body was laid in the tomb, did not merely come alive again, but he was raised up by God himself, not like Lazarus to mortal life, but to eternal majesty, and this majesty was in contrast with his humiliation and could only be gained through it. And in this grand *Anastasis*—that is the Greek word for Resurrection—there are first, as presuppositions, the high claims that Jesus made, and the ignominy, suffering, and death that seemed to falsify them; then there are the acts of power that followed, the self-raising from the dead, the resurrection body and appearances, the return of confidence to the Apostles, the ascension into heaven, and the being set down on the right hand of God; then there are the effects in a new sense of power human and divine, a revival not only of Christ's life but of the life of his disciples, a new beginning, a forgiveness of sins, the foundation of the Church, a life in God with the resurrection of the body as its corollary, and a vivid hope of everlasting joy. When the Resurrection was first preached, it meant all these things, as you can see plainly enough from the Acts of Apostles and the sermons there of St. Peter and St. Paul, though the word itself applied in strictness only to the rising from the tomb and the appearances which proved it.

Yes, but did these appearances prove anything more than the fact of the rising from the tomb, if they proved that? Phlegon asked. Did all that you say follow logically from this?

No, Philologus answered. It did not follow logically, although there was reason in it. But the Apostles were in a state far beyond logic, a mixture of relief and faith and joy and confidence which were their own verification, or in their minds at least could need no verification. It simply had that effect upon them, though they had not reckoned upon such an effect, and no more could we.

Then are we entitled to maintain what they maintained?

Certainly, if we can experience their conviction, and then justify it. That is how it works, and not the other way round. You don't have to prove the resurrection first and then feel convinced of it. You feel convinced of it, and then set about to defend your conviction. God expects that of you, if he has given you the brains to do it. And I suppose that in actual fact that is how most of the things of the Spirit work, and it occurs to me that we might find a parallel at a somewhat lower level in Tragedy. You would not suppose beforehand that a tragedy would give you satisfaction and indeed serenity, but, if it is properly managed, as by Sophocles and sometimes by Shakespeare, that is just what it does do. And in a sense the Christian religion is a tragedy of this sort, though it is a tragedy with a happy ending—the only real one that there is, it may be. Christianity in all that it calls the Resurrection gives the true answer to human life as a whole, just as Tragedy

124

gives the true answer to certain aspects of life. They are both a justification of God and man, of God who is all Resurrection and Life, and of man whose sole end is the Vision of God.

We are getting into something which sounds like a mixture of aesthetics and the metaphysical, Patrobas said. I feel, my dear Philologus, that you could write a very nice book about it. But I do not think that as a party here and now we are altogether suited to contend with it. Let me ask a pedantic, or at least a pedestrian, question. What does the Greek word Anastasis actually mean?

It means so many things, doesn't it? It is just the noun formed from a very common verb which covers most of what we mean by raising up and rising up and even getting up. But it sometimes adds to these a further idea, as if you were to say to someone, Get up and be gone. It means uprooting and something like transportation. It also has an underlying notion of renewal. So it was quite a natural word to use for Resurrection, and then as a technical word in the preaching of the Christian religion for all that great series of events which form the conclusion, or one might almost say the second and greater half of the Gospel. I think one might reckon Anastasis to be the most original and emphatic word in the vocabulary of the Apostles. The Athenians, when St. Paul preached to them, got the idea that he was trying to commend to them two new divinities, a god called Jesus and a goddess called Anastasis. But it has often been observed that St. Paul made no impression by his preaching at Athens, and the reason was that he thought it necessary to try, in the presence of such an intellectual gathering, to put arguments before them, and this question of the Resurrection is just where arguments won't work. There is of course a logical and critical approach to the Resurrection, as there is to other aspects of our religion, and a theology to be got out of it, but these will only serve to forge tools for the Christian teacher, and he must have the skill to employ them effectively; they don't work for themselves. You can see that well enough in the fifteenth chapter of the First Corinthians, where the arguments are interesting but not decisive. The decisive part is the correspondence of the Resurrection of Christ with all the expectations which seem most significant in human life. If nothing attains to lasting glory in this life, nevertheless everything seems to point to it, and the Resurrection seemed to show the way for sure to glory.

Glory is a fine word, Phlegon said. But what is glory? I remember somewhere in the New Testament it says something about *rejoicing in the hope of the glory of God*, but what am I to hope for? How am I to rejoice?

The place is in the Epistle to the Romans, Philologus answered. And Glory certainly is a fine word in English, and so is Gloire in French, and so is Gloria in Latin, where the other two come from. In Latin the original notion, it is thought, is of what men are heard to say of someone, rumour or fame that is, and then of great fame, and then of the brilliant deeds which bring great fame; and in English glory always points to the height of fame or honour. But glory has an added meaning, because in the New Testament it translates a Greek word of special significance. That word is *doxa*, from which we get orthodox, and paradox, and doxology. It starts by meaning that which appears to be true, therefore an opinion, with a suggestion that it is no more than an opinion. But then it may come to mean a settled opinion, a decision, though this is often called a *dogma* rather than a doxa. But doxa also goes off in another direction and means an opinion or estimate of a person, his reputation, then a specially good reputation, then fame, then glory much in the Latin sense. Then it comes to have a notion of brilliance or brightness about it, and was thought suitable in the Septuagint to describe the glory of God, which so often appears in the Old Testament under the figure or in the form of a bright light, whether on the top of a mountain, or in the Tabernacle, or in a vision. And from thence the glory of God means in general the splendour and majesty of God, whether seen in the court of Heaven or in the person of Jesus Christ. In the old days a picture of the heavenly hosts attending upon God was called a 'Glory', just as a picture of the Day of Judgment was called a 'Doom'. A great Glory of this kind is described in a famous passage of Isaiah :

In the year that king Uzziah died I saw also the Lord sitting upon a throne, high and lifted up, and his train filled the temple. Above it stood the seraphims : each one had six wings : with twain he covered his face, and with twain he covered his feet, and with twain he did fly. And one cried unto another, and said, Holy, holy, holy, is the Lord of Hosts : the whole earth is full of his glory.

And what we may call a Christian glory is all gathered up in a single, wonderful sentence of St. Paul:

> *God, who commanded the light to shine out of darkness, hath shined in our hearts, to give the light of the knowledge of the glory of God in the face of Jesus Christ.*

This idea of the glory of God in the face of Jesus Christ looks back to the brightness of Moses' face after he had been with God—Paul calls that brightness doxa—and it looks forward to that interchange of glory between the Father and the Son which St. John makes so much of, as for example in the words of Jesus after Judas Iscariot went out to betray him: *Now is the Son of Man glorified, and God is glorified in him. If God be glorified in him, God shall also glorify him in himself.* And there are of course other similar passages.

But indeed, Philologus continued, the whole Bible is full of the glory of God. We glorify him, that is to say, we attribute glory to him, and we hope to come to glory, which is nothing else than to come to him. And although St. Paul speaks of God *dwelling in the light which no man can approach unto,* St. Peter says he *has called us out of darkness into his marvellous light.* And both of course are right. In Dante's Paradise there are no colours, only varying intensity of light, yet no one has come nearer to describing the confines of the glory in which the life of the world to come is to be lived. Dante ends with the testimony that at last 'strength failed at this high fantasy'. And perhaps it is the failure of speech at the climax of such fantasy or vision that has made Glory one of the few words that have had almost no misuse and possess undiminished the power to signify the light of Christ in God and Man.

There was a pause, and in the silence each of us became aware that it was growing dark. Patrobas, murmuring to himself something about 'John Keble's lines', began quietly to recite the old Greek hymn 'at the lighting of the lamps':

> *Hail, gladdening Light, of his pure glory pour'd*
> *Who is the Immortal Father, Heavenly, Blest,*
> *Holiest of Holies, Jesus Christ our Lord.*

And then Hermas and Hermes began, as twins sometimes will, to speak together word for word:
127

Now we are come to the sun's hour of rest,
  The lights of evening round us shine.
We hymn the Father, Son and Holy Spirit Divine.

And Philologus said, I wish we could all sing this together, but I do not know that we few should make much of singing a hymn or any sort of music here in the open. Yet perhaps such a talk as we have had and the wish to learn and know are themselves a kind of hymn, acceptable to the Father and the Son and the Holy Spirit of God.

And Phlegon said, I am afraid I was sometimes very impatient. I was rather objectionable.

And Philologus said, You and Asyncritus are young, and it becomes you to be over-eager. And if by objectionable you mean full of objections, what after all would discussion amount to without someone who was that?

THE KING'S INSTITUTE
THE CHURCH ON THE WAY